FLAMES IN TH

FLAMES IN THE SKY

Pierre Clostermann
D.S.O., D.F.C.

Translated by OLIVER BERTHOUD

SILVERTAIL BOOKS • *London*

To my comrades in the air who died to wipe out past mistakes – mistakes which were not theirs. To those who may yet have to pay for new, and yet still the same mistakes by the Great who refuse to believe the lessons of the past.

CONTENTS

Preface   1

1 Prelude   5

2 Pearl Harbor and Bataan   14

   Pearl Harbor   15

   Bataan Peninsula   28

   Note on the Zero   45

3 A Day in Malta   56

   A Day in Malta   57

4 Admiral Yamamoto   83

   Note on the Lockheed P-38 'Lightning'   99

5 Colonel Pijeaud   106

6 Flames over Warsaw   122

7 Max Guedj   136

   Note on the Mosquito   160

8 The Twilight of the Gods   167

   Note on the Messerschmitt 262   180

9 Under The Sign of the Divine Wind   184

   Notes on the Baka, the German 'Natter',

   the Myrt and the George   206

PREFACE

In 1946 I began to realise a project which I had set my heart on as early as 1940, the History of the War in the Air. I have worked through hundreds and thousands of documents from the archives of the Luftwaffe, the Air Ministry and the United States Navy and Army Air Forces. I have read roughly speaking all the translations of Japanese documents collected together by the Pentagon in Washington, all the books published in America, France, England, Switzerland, Italy and Spain. Already the fruits of five years of patient research have accumulated, and in a few months, if events permit, the book will be ready.

It is now, nearly at the end of this task, that I have suddenly become aware of the very grave danger to which the historian of this war is exposed by the very nature of the vast documentation at his disposal. When everything had been digested, classified, annotated, drafted, I realised that out of that sum total of individual exploits, acts of courage, often anonymous, sacrifices by men of every race and creed, nothing is left in the end but a mass of papers, maps, photos, figures and statistics.

The human lessons are hidden by the strategic lessons. The skill of human hands and the bravery of human hearts disappear in the cold-blooded study of materials and technique. Heroism is masked behind the communiqués and the operational reports. And yet what stories of sublime courage and energy the historian discovers as he pores over the columns of figures in the frightening balance-sheet of modern air war.

Debit . . . credit . . . aircraft lost . . . tons of bombs . . . enemy destroyed . . . ships sunk . . . killed . . . wounded . . . missing . . . total . . . year . . . Is nothing to emerge from the gigantic drama of the 1939-45 war but blue-prints and reports on industrial organisation? Such an idea is revolting. Are we to forget that under the tons of debris in the devastated towns, homes were crushed by the bombs? Are we to forget that under the charred and twisted wreckage of aircraft it was human flesh burnt?

It was men who suffered in the sky as they handled those masterpieces of modern technique. It was men who perished in terrible suffering to carry out the plans of the strategists. It was men who sacrificed themselves so that others might live. It was men, too, who went through hell to redeem the military and political mistakes of some and save the honour of others.

Is it by making people study graphs and curves of consumption that we shall teach them to hate war and to respect those who have been through it?

That is why I felt I must, here and now, relate these few stones of flying men, culled from among hundreds and thousands of others which will be buried in ministerial archives and historical research departments. They are neither finer nor stranger than those which will remain unknown. I have chosen them rather haphazardly, merely because they are typical of certain phases of the war and of certain theatres of operations. Each of these stories gives the 'feel' of a particular aspect of the war in varying latitudes and circumstances.

Their only common factor is the courage and idealism of those whose lives they relate, and they show above all that, under different guises, the highest virtues of man are the prerogative of no single nation.

In each of these stories I have begun with a brief sketch of the main lines of the campaign in question, so that the reader can see the action involved in its right perspective and against the right background. Since for a great number of readers some of the campaigns—that in the Pacific, for instance—were in the nature of things rather distant, I have thought it advisable describe also those important actors, the aircraft themselves.

For a pilot, every plane has its own personality, which always reflects that of its designers and colours the mentality of those who take it into action.

The Spitfire, for instance, is typically British. Temperate, a perfect compromise of all the qualities required of a fighter, ideally suited to its task of defence. An essentially reasonable piece of machinery, conceived by cool, precise brains and built by conscientious hands. The Spitfire left such an imprint on those who flew it that when they changed to other types they found it very hard to get acclimatised.

Certain aircraft will also go down to history as classics, typifying their epoch. The 1914-18 war calls to mind the Spad, the Breguet 14, the de Havilland DH-4, the Fokker and the Gotha. My generation, i.e. the 1939-45 generation, will immediately think of the 'Spit,' the Morane 406, the Stuka, the Messerschmitt 109, the Mosquito, the Yak, the Zero, the Fortress and the two-tailed Lightning.

Each of these planes had its tale of technical troubles, disappointments and successes, of tactics imposed upon it by its design, and above all of affection or dislike of those who flew it.

PIERRE CLOSTERMANN

CHAPTER ONE

PRELUDE

12th May 1940, Maestricht

'DURING the night and in the early morning there were important enemy movements in the Ardennes region and towards the West. The columns include bridging crews. Large motorised armoured forces are on the march towards the Meuse coming respectively from DINAN, GIVET and NEUFCHATEAU.

'Our reconnaissance reports in addition strong columns on the roads on the general axis MAESTRICHT-TONGRES.'

Intelligence Summary, 12th May 1940

The storm coming from the East spread its flood over Flanders and the North of France. The hordes of refugees on the march ran up against our tangled and already disorganised military convoys coming up to stem the enemy tide. And already, infiltrating through the cracks in our hills, spreading over the plains, by-passing the towns, driving onward on a rattle of tracks and a stench of diesels, the Panzer divisions were about to fall upon France.

Drifting on the east wind, the long white condensation trails criss-crossed the blue spring sky, and over the green countryside stretched the shadow of the long black smoke-trails of the invasion.

The men, huddled in the ditches, shook their fists at the sky: 'The swine!'

The swine were the Stukas, tumbling down like an avalanche. First, a few black spots up there in the sky and a distant roar, then down they spiralled one after the other, and above the crescendo of the engines came the scream of the bombs.

The W-shaped wings with their flaps and dive-brakes, perched on the two slender legs of the undercarriage, the yawning gape of the radiator—all that came smack down into your eyes with a roar like the Day of Judgment. The men were left dazed and quivering.

A few cars were burning on the road and from some useless overturned B-2 came a whiff of burnt rubber and roasted flesh.

'The swine!'

And that included their own aircraft, whose wings they could see burning in a field; and also those who were getting massacred high up and far away, trying to make some impression on this terror which flowed over the roads and fell upon them from the sky.

The long Dornier 17s were still slipping westwards, and from the bellies of the serried squadrons of Heinkel IIIs fell the sticks of bombs, pirouetting down to smash stations and villages. Up above, the angry buzz of the Messerschmitt 110s keeping watch and, all around, the clumps of Messerschmitt 109s with their yellow bellies and their clipped wings, scouring the sky. Black crosses, nothing but black crosses.

In spite of that, at every cross-road in the villages submerged by the armoured columns, on the banks of the Meuse, perched on the piles of the demolished bridges, the long tubes of the German 37-mm. guns were springing up, pointing skywards. At road junctions the half-tracks of the flak service were taking up position and setting up their multiple 20-mm. mountings. The clips of shells were lined up by the roadsides and the spotters kept a look out from the banks, rangefinders at the ready.

It was at Maestricht that the first blow of the battering-ram fell. The narrow streets of the little Dutch town overflowed with the continuous flood of tanks and trucks, crawling along the banks of the Meuse to the pontoon bridge thrown across alongside the collapsed railway viaduct by the German engineers. All that swarm of vehicles flooded on to the roads to Tongres and Bilsen and poured in. an endless stream over the intact bridges across the Albert Canal at Veldwezelt and Vroenhoven. A few miles to the south, the fort of Eben-Emael, its glacis covered with variegated parachutes and capped with smoke, had just succumbed. The haggard defenders came stumbling out of the shattered casemates and staggered down to the plain, picking their way between the carcasses of the gliders and covered by the submachine-guns of the enemy parachutists. On the dark waters of the canal the empty rubber dinghies of the special assault troops drifted away.

Inside those few square miles, bounded to the west by the Albert Canal—that gigantic and useless anti-tank ditch—to the north by the Meuse and the Maestricht Canal and to the southeast by the Jaar, meandering through the flooded fields, seven Panzer divisions concentrated.

Directed one by one, by the sweat and dust-covered Wehrmacht traffic policemen; over the bridges still standing the tanks and the six-wheeled armoured cars slowly crossed, their long antennae waving. But once over, the tanks accelerated in a roar of exhausts, churning up the macadam with their steel tracks. The impregnable defences had crumbled, the infallible plans had been torn to shreds, the comprehensive measures had been swept aside.

It was then, to put off the inevitable, that our fighters and bombers were cruelly thrown into the furnace, in pathetic driblets. Who could have seen them, lost as they were in the vast sky? Those poor French planes which took off on clear mornings in May 1940 and never came back, pounced on by the Messerschmitts or picked off by the flak! Yes, the flak. For already this was a nightmare for the pilots, the little guns of the automatic flak with their long venomous barrels spitting up strings of steel pearls which sliced off your wings and blinded you. Every German battalion brought reinforcements to the flak as it passed. The quadruple 20-mm. anchored themselves between the poplars on the banks and more 37-mm. were unloaded from the trucks. The gun crews in shirt sleeves piled up the ammunition and stumbled over the heaps of empties. The observation post was perched high up the chimney of some brickworks and the battery commanders scanned the Meuse valley through their glasses. There was a flak emplacement every fifty yards along the three miles of the canal from the Vroenhoven bridge to the Veldwezelt bridge. Protected by them, the convoys of troop-laden trucks passed through in an endless stream. There was no risk anyway, for the Luftwaffe was mistress of the sky.

The two previous alerts had proved it. The Belgian Fairey Battles of the Hepcée flight, reinforced by the Pierre flight, had taken off from Aeltre between Ghent and Bruges. The three sections of three aircraft dived through a terrific flak barrage, only to be picked up by the watchful Messerschmitts. Six planes out of the nine were shot down. With sublime courage two pilots, Captain Glorie and Sergeant Delvigne, whose bombs had not fallen on the first run over the target, came back a second time into the furnace and crashed in flames. The bridges were still intact. A few hours later the R.A.F. had a try. The eight Hurricanes of No. 1 squadron, commanded by Squadron-Leader 'Bull' Halahan, took off to keep the Messerschmitts out of the way, while six Fairey Battles of Bomber Command tried to destroy at least the Veldwezelt bridge. They ran into the Messerschmitt 109s from Aix-la-Chapelle, Hehn, Hohenbudberg, Gladbach and Vogelsand, more than 120 fighters. The rendezvous with the bombers was at 9.15. It was 9.12. Three minutes left to clear the way for the bombers. The Hurricanes went for the Messerschmitts bald-headed and were soon struggling heroically against the angry pack. Halahan's plane exploded and his parachute opened in the nick of time over the canal. F/O Lewis came down soon after. Three Messerschmitt 109s were destroyed, but the R.A.F. fighters were overcome by superior numbers and four others were shot down.

The diversion did, however, produce the desired effect. The six Battles dived straight into the flak, straightening out a few yards from the bridge. Three bombs scored hits, but three plants were shot down. A fourth, piloted by F/Lt. Garland, the Flight Leader, crashed straight into the bridge, which collapsed in a shower of spray. The fifth spiralled down, one wing torn off.

The sixth managed to get home, escorted by the two surviving Hurricanes.

The fields round about were strewn with charred carcases of aircraft—crumpled wings, shattered fuselages, pathetic bits of aluminium surrounded by circles of dead grass, blackened by oil and flames from the gutted fuel-tanks. Occasionally a few German sappers would hastily dig a trench where the poor smashed bodies of the pilots were laid, wrapped in the silk of their parachutes.

Then once again the white alarm rockets, announcing a new sacrifice. Blasts on whistles and the shrill hooters of the Flugalarm. Before the aircraft were even visible the 200 barrels of the flak reared up and opened fire—a prodigious drum-roll as a prelude to the execution.

Wreaths of smoke ran along the tow-paths and a thousand dazzling parabolas of 20-mm. tracer shells formed a mosaic of black and grey bursts. The trucks had stopped. The soldiers in their field-grey clung to the running-boards and looked round questioningly. Suddenly the drivers switched off and jumped into the ditches, the men crouched down behind the trees.

Six aircraft swept up like whirlwinds from behind the brick steeples of Maestricht. They were the Breguet 693s of Fighter Squadron 1/54—mid-wing monoplanes with twin Gnome-Rhone engines, fuselages shaped like tadpoles and twin fins set high on the tailplanes. Starting from a perfect right echelon formation, they fanned out in a deafening roar. Each aircraft climbed steeply through the streams of tracer, its identification markings showing up clearly on the grey fuselage. They levelled out, then dived hell for leather, bomb bays open. The first, No. 49, one engine already in flames, let go its six light bombs, which ricochetted and exploded among the camouflaged lorries. Like a comet dragging a long fiery tail it turned and its heroic pilot came back, enfilading the road with his cannon and his fixed machine-guns. Rolling from side to side, out of control, it broke away and. crashed in a terrific shower of sparks on top of a group of armoured cars which were ground into the dust by the impact of the six-ton plane going at 300 m.p.h.

Breguet No. 21 came in flat out, let go its bombs and then levelled out over the canal, hugging the water and pursued by black bursts. On the way it machine-gunned two flak emplacements, whose crews collapsed over the guns. It got away.

The third plane attacked through the incandescent ribbons which scored the sky. The flak guns strewed its path with thousands of fragments of steel. Among the crash of the bombs and the roar of engines four sharp metallic cracks rang out—four hits on the slender wings, four trails of smoke. The Breguet immediately burst into flames like a torch. The pilot switched off his engines, lowered his flaps, and went into a violent sideslip and belly-landed in a marshy field with a scream of metal.

There was a lull in the flak. The gunners looked round wondering 'what next?' A new flight of three Breguets, Nos. 7, 9 and 4 which had feinted towards Tongres, came back at right angles to the congested enemy columns, so low that they seemed be slipping from one field into the next. Taking advantage of the lull, they shot between the trees, dropped their bombs and let fly with their guns, and then jumped the row of poplars. But the flak had the last word all the same, for two of them were disgorging a heavy stream of black smoke.

More Breguets arrived, soon caught in the impenetrable meshes of the flak. The wings of No. 14 were torn to ribbons, and the machine, its ailerons gone, and now quite unmanageable, crashed into the trees by the roadside, bounced, and hit the ground/in a cloud of dust which was soon fringed with flame.

No. 19, a river of fire twenty yards long issuing from its punctured tanks, suddenly climbed vertically and two dark shapes emerged from the cockpit and started spinning down— two parachutes opened out, apparently fixed in space while the plane flicked over and went into a spin.

The last of the Breguets, No. 22, engines flat out, dived desperately in turn, multi-coloured tracer whipping under its fuselage. It dropped its bombs diagonally across a park of artillery tractors. Then it was hit, wobbled, and fragments of aluminium tom off by the bullets fluttered in its slipstream, but miraculously it got through and vanished into the dense smoke of the fires raging all along the road.

That was the end. A hundred or so vehicles were blazing away on the road, their burning fuel eating into the tar. The sky was bespattered with bursts in thick clumps and criss-crossed with grey smoke-trails. Through the roar of the column getting under way could be heard from the Tongres direction the muffled rattle of the flak baying after the surviving Breguet. Once again the tanks and trucks were irresistibly on the move. Eight aircraft for four minutes' respite!

The flak stayed in position, and the sacrifice went on. In the course of the afternoon the R.A.F., following the heroic French fighter-pilots from 1/54, made another effort to halt the avalanche of enemy armour from Maestricht. Collecting all its available Fairey Battles, it sent them into the fray. Sixty-seven planes started—thirty-one came through, most of them so severely damaged that they were unable to get back to England. Later on it was the turn of the Lioré-et-Olivier 45s, while our Curtiss's, our Dewoitines and our Moranes tried to get their teeth into the formations of Dorniers. The Messerschmitts' death-dance went on in our skies just the same. A thousand successes, but also five hundred pilots massacred because they were too few and it was too late.

The flames spread from one sky to another—from the yellow plains of Poland to the green Vosges, from the soot of London to the snows of Russia and from the blue of the Pacific to the ice of Alaska . . . too little—too late!

CHAPTER TWO

PEARL HARBOR AND BATAAN

'Too little, too late'

THE tragedy of France and the Low Countries, the result of our superiority complex, improvisation, complacency, administrative chaos and improvidence, was to be repeated for the Americans when the Japanese attacked on 7th December 1941.

There, too, cheese-paring while the spectre of war loomed large on the horizon, the hope of a problematical appeasement by dint of concessions, outworn tactical and strategical ideas, were to exact a heavy price in unnecessary sacrifices and lost lives.

Luckily for the United States, just as England had the Channel, they had the vast Pacific Ocean between their territory, their factories and their people and the Empire of the Rising Sun. We French had only the Rhine and the Meuse.

The Pearl Harbor disaster, which has been the subject of the most gigantic official enquiry in history—the record of the proceedings runs to over 20,000 pages—deserves a book to itself. The mystery of the Japanese code, of President Roosevelt's foreknowledge of the enemy plans, of all that went on in the White House, will presumably one day be revealed.

That is not the object of this story, but nevertheless certain features of that Japanese operation must be mentioned and also a brief sketch made of the air battles over the Philippines in order that the reader may appreciate the epic story of the 24th Interceptor Group of the U.S.A.F. in Bataan, from Christmas 1941 to the end of March 1942.

PEARL HARBOR

7th December 1941

It was Sunday morning—the first Sunday after payday for the G.I.s and sailors of the base. All night the dance halls and bars of Pearl Harbor had been turning people away. The Fleet had come in the day before—apart from the aircraft-carriers—and Hawaii had been the scene of the usual junketings on the first Saturday in the month.

There were few people still up at 3.45 a.m., apart from the poker addicts and those wending their way back to their Mess.

In a tent on a hillside overlooking the misty sea an alarm-clock went off. Technical Corporal 3rd Class Joe Lockard and Private George Elliot climbed grumbling out of their damp blankets and after a quick wash went to their post in the chilly morning air.

By their tent stood a large square steel trailer with narrow slatted windows. On the roof, covered with a tarpaulin which the men carefully removed, was a large parabolic aerial shaped like an electric bowl fire. It was one of the three SCR 260-B experimental radar sets which had arrived from England. Nobody had much faith in this queer British contraption. Joe

Lockard, an amateur radio fan in private life, was the only one—
or at any rate one of the few—for whom the apparatus was now
practically an open book.

The radar sets had arrived in July and had been on the go
continuously from 10th November to 3rd December whenever
an 'alarm' warning had been given. Handled as they were by
inexpert crews, they had begun to go wrong and there were now
only three spare cathode-ray tubes. H.Q. had decided to use
them only from one hour before dawn till one hour after sunrise, i.e. about from 4 to 7 a.m.

It wasn't much fun being on duty in this remote spot and in
those conditions while the other fellows had all the Hawaii hot-
spots at their disposal and lived in air-conditioned barracks.

They had switched on and the radar was warming up. Lockard
was keeping an eye on the hypnotising dance of the oscilloscope.
He busied himself plotting the permanent interference, to hand
in at the next weekly inspection—if the officer on duty didn't
forget. Now and then Elliot asked if there weren't at long last
any blips to see. Lockard did not even bother to reply. Blips?
What blips? There were never any planes up, so there couldn't
be any blips—especially on a Sunday!

The radiant sun dispersed the mist and rose over the peaceful,
flower-decked island.

At 6.45 Lockard suddenly saw a very faint blip appear on the
extreme edge of the screen, right at the top. Bearing 330 degrees.
At 6.55 the blip, which seemed to be zigzagging slowly, coming
back on itself and then going north again, became quite clear for
a moment.

Lockard, without warning Elliot, who was busy outside with the generator, put a call through to Control over the normal line. After a five-minute wait he was put through to a duty officer who took a dim view of the whole thing and told him pretty sharply to mind his own business.

Out of sense of duty Lockard made a note of the tracks and the times. At 6.58 the blip, still very faint, disappeared completely. At 7 o'clock, as per instructions, Lockard switched off and locked up the trailer. The two men stood waiting for the truck which was to take them back to the Mess for breakfast, when they heard the phone go. It was to tell them they couldn't get picked up till 7.30.

Lockard, furious, and having nothing better to do, went back to his radar and switched it on again, while Elliot put a shine on his shoes in a corner.

7.02—'Hi, George, come over here, quick!'

Elliot rushed over.

'Look!'

A miracle! For the first time for three months since they had been looking after that radar set, here was an honest-to-goodness blip, perfectly sharp. The big transparent green blip was moving fast southwards, towards Hawaii.

'Plot it!'

Elliot quickly placed a round sheet of transparent squared paper over the map, stuck a pin through the middle over where their station was, and got ready to take down the dope.

'7.02. Point 130. That was where they were when I first saw them!'

Probably Navy planes, thought Elliot, from an aircraft-carrier on manoeuvres out at sea, bringing ashore officers who wanted to spend a Sunday with their families. But they generally operated south of the island.

'Take down—7.04—132.'

Elliot did a quick calculation on a special slide-rule. The planes were going about 225 m.p.h. Lockard kept his eye on the bright dot quivering on the screen and hesitated. Would he get bawled out again? He unhooked the special phone on the direct line to Control at Fort Shafter, reserved for urgent messages. Only after furiously winding the handle for several minutes did he hear the receiver being lifted at the other end. He recognised the voice.

'Hullo, Macdonald? Is that you, Joe?'

'Yeah.'

'Lockard here, from Opona Station. Find me someone at Central Control, it's very important.'

'There ain't no one here any more. The place shuts at seven, didn't you know?'

'Say, listen, Macdonald, be a pal and find me an officer, any one will do.'

Three minutes passed, while the blips got bigger and started to split up as they got nearer. Then a curt voice spoke in the phone:

'Lieutenant Tyler here, duty officer.'

'Lockard here, Lieutenant, with the SCR at Opona. I have spotted an important formation of planes making for Hawaii. At 0702 hours they were 136 miles away, and bearing zero to 10 degrees.'

'H'm'—The voice was perplexed and hesitant. 'O.K. I've got it. Don't worry. It's O.K.' The duty officer hung up.

At 7.28 the signs got lost in the fringe of permanent blips. The formation of aircraft was only twenty-two miles away. At 7.30 the truck picked up Elliot and Lockard, but they were fated not to get their breakfast that day.

At 7.57, on the glass-fronted balcony of the tall control tower on Hickham airfield, overlooking the naval base, Colonel Bertholf, who was worrying about the arrival of sixteen Flying Fortresses coming from San Francisco, suddenly leaped to his ; feet. In his binoculars he could see a long line of black dots—aircraft—approaching Kanai. There were about fifty of them, all single-engined.

The Colonel turned to the controller and asked him if they were Navy aircraft. Without even looking up he answered that it was unlikely, so early, on a Sunday morning.

A few moments later the planes began to peel off one by one and dive on Pearl Harbor. Showers of spray arose among the ships of the line jammed tightly together and powerless to move.

It was the Japs![1]

At six in the morning Vice-Admiral C. Nagumo—commanding the First Air Fleet detailed for the attack on Pearl

---

[1] In addition to the radar information, two other facts ought to have alerted Pearl Harbor. At 6.51 a Japanese midget submarine was sunk, just after coming into the fairway, by the destroyer *Ward*, which immediately sent in a signal. At 6.53 the control room on the aircraft-carrier *Enterprise* heard the pilot of one of it patrolling aircraft sent over Ford island, Ensign Manoel Gonzales, yell: 'Don't shoot. I'm American. Christ!' The Zeros were shooting him down.

Unfortunately no one was in command at Pearl Harbor. Admiral Stark and General Short each kept a jealous eye on the other Service, stuck to his own planes, and tried to palm off all the dirty jobs on to the other.

Harbor—had hoisted the 'Z' flag on the mast of the aircraft-carrier *Akagi*. It was the original flag hoisted by Togo at Tsushima in 1905 when he won the first great naval battle of modern times, brought on board the flagship in a lacquer and gold casket.

'Z'—attack!

To fulfil his mission Nagumo had under his command six aircraft-carriers protected by nine destroyers, two heavy cruisers and two battleships. His six aircraft-carriers, with their romantic names, were: the *Akagi* (Red Castle), the *Shokaku* (Climbing Crane), the *Zuikaku* (Happy Crane), the *Kaga* (Increasing Joy), the *Soryu* (Green Dragon) and the *Hiryu* (Flying Paragon).

The squadron's senior navigation officer had surpassed himself, in spite of the bad weather which had prevented him from verifying his positions and his time schedule by the stars. At zero hour the exact position for launching the attack—lat. 26° N. long. 128° N.—had been reached.

The first wave comprised ninety Kates[2] (forty equipped with special torpedoes driven by oxygen, and the others with 1000-lb. bombs) and fifty Val dive-bombers, the whole escorted by fifty Zeros. This first formation was entrusted with the principal task, i.e. the sinking of the American battle fleet.

The second wave, whose task was to neutralise the airfields, comprised fifty Kates, eighty Vals and forty Zeros.

At 7.56 the war between the United States and Japan began.

---

[2] These code-names were not given until later in the war, but are used here for convenience. The planes were Aichi Type 99 (Val); Nakajima Type 97 (Kate); and Mitsubishi Type O (Zeke, generally known as Zero).

In the officers' club at the great Wheeler airfield a poker game was just finishing. The previous evening—Saturday, 6th December—there had been a dinner-dance and the game had begun at 1 a.m., when most of the guests went home. At 6 in the morning play was still going on at one solitary table, and half an hour later two young Air Force Lieutenants, cleaned out to the last cent by three Navy officers, went out for a breath of air.

What was there to do so early on a Sunday morning? Lieutenants Welch and Taylor were muzzy with alcohol and cigarette smoke. They decided to have an invigorating bathe in the sea, followed by a few hours' sleep on the warm sands of Haleiwa beach by their airfield. Their car was the only one left in the car park. In front of them stretched the runways or Wheeler Field covered with aircraft. For a moment they admired the seventy-five magnificent Curtiss P-40s, just out of their crates, parked nose to nose and wing to wing to prevent possible sabotage by Japanese agents. In front of them two sentries were pacing up and down.

Just as Taylor was slamming the door of the Ford, bought second-hand and painted bright orange—they were young—a formation of planes swooped over the hangars with a thunder of exploding bombs. For the fraction of a second the young men sat paralysed, but they sprang into action soon enough when a hail of bullets bespattered them with asphalt from the road. It was only then that they saw the red Japanese discs on the elliptic wings of one of the planes—a small squat monoplane with fixed undercarriage.

'Jesus, the Japs! It's a dive-bomber!'

Welch backed his car viciously into the shelter of the club verandah and leapt to the telephone in the hall, while bullets were sending the tiles flying. He called up his unit.

'Get two P-40s ready—mine and Taylor's. Load up—it's not a gag, the Japs are here! Get going.'

He hung up, rushed out past the petrified Mess staff, who were cowering behind armchairs, tripped over a body and jumped into his car. Foot hard down on the accelerator, cursing his stupidity for having the car painted such a conspicuous colour, he roared along the twisting but luckily empty road at eighty miles an hour. The few cars he met were stationary, their occupants prudently lying in the ditches— including the traffic M.P.s apparently, as they saw three unattended red motorcycles propped up against some telegraph poles. No danger of a charge for speeding, anyway, and they took their corners on two wheels.

The nine miles took them less than ten minutes and on the way they were strafed—and missed—three times by the Japs. On the airfield they skidded to a halt on the damp grass and ran towards their planes. The fitters jumped down from their cock-pits and a private staggered up with their parachutes, helmets and gloves. The engines were already running.

One minute later the two Curtiss's took off wing-tip to wing-tip and plunged into the low clouds coming in from the sea.

Haleiwa, tucked away at the northern extremity of the island in a hollow in the hills and covered by a providential layer of cloud, had miraculously escaped the attention of the Vals and Zeros, which had all been attracted by the enormous fires at

Pearl Harbor and Hickham Field in the south. It is true that the well-informed Japanese knew it was a tiny training-field, where planes only came for shooting practice. As a matter of fact, 47 Squadron with its four P-36s and its fourteen P-40s had been there no more than a few days.

In all only seven fighters—and each one on his own initiative, like Welch and Taylor—managed to get into the air and intercept. Between them they brought down twelve Japs, whom they caught by surprise. Welch alone bagged four. However, each time they came up against Zeros instead of Vals they were outclassed. Lieutenants Christiansen, Whiteman, Bishop, Gordon Sterling, Dains and finally Taylor, Welch's friend, were all brought down in this way.

Lieutenant Welch, who managed to survive not only the Zeros but also the threat of a court-martial for having taken off without orders, received the D.S.C. a fortnight later. Subsequently, when the reports were gone through in Washington and General Arnold saw that Welch had taken off no fewer than three times— the last time, with two machine-guns out of four out of action, he had baled out—he recommended him for the Congressional Medal of Honour.

It was said at the time that the Air Officer Commanding in Pearl Harbor opposed the recommendation because Welch had taken off without orders. But finally, in spite of his outstanding war record, Welch was never awarded this high decoration.

At 10.15 on the 7th of December it was all over in Hawaii. Those responsible for the defence of the island got their stories ready, knowing that they would have to account for what had happened, and that scapegoats would have to be found for public opinion to tear to pieces.

Out of eight battleships in the harbour, five were sunk and three very badly damaged. At Kanehoe, the Naval air-base, out of thirty-six PBY Catalinas, large twin-engined long-range flying boats, twenty-seven were destroyed and six so seriously damaged as to be beyond repair. Only the three which were on patrol south of the island at the time of the attack escaped.

At Ewa, also a Navy air-base, there were eleven Wildcat fighters, thirty-two observation planes and six DC-3 transports. Fifteen Zeros, by machine-gun fire alone, in four minutes destroyed nine fighters, eighteen observation planes and all six transports.

The Army Air Force had, at 7 a.m., 221 good war-planes, dispersed on the three main airfields, Hickham, Wheeler and Bellows Fields, and the small satellite field at Haleiwa. Three hours later it had lost: eight B-17 Flying Fortresses, twenty-two B-18s and seven A-20s, all bombers. What was particularly serious was that every single fighter had been destroyed—sixty-two P-40Bs, eleven P-40Cs, twenty-three P-36s and nine P-26s. Every single plane, whether Navy or Army, which had escaped was damaged.

The Japanese had lost nine planes in the first wave and twenty-one in the second, a loss of thirty planes to put out of action 75 per cent, of the total American naval and air forces in the Pacific. If the White House wanted the American people to be shaken out of its apathy, then it got what it wanted with a vengeance.

A few hours after the blow at Pearl Harbor, at the other end of the Pacific, the Japanese hurled themselves with irresistible ferocity on the Philippines and Singapore. There, too, they had calmly gone ahead with their preparations amid the general somnolence.

Twice, on 24th and 25th November, brazenly and in broad daylight, two Japanese reconnaissance planes had photographed from a height of 23,000 feet every American airfield in the Philippines.

The interpretation of the photos revealed the presence of scarcely 300 American aircraft, instead of the 900 the Japanese were expecting. This considerably relieved Admiral Tsukahara, in command of the 11th Imperial Air Fleet, which was earmarked for these operations. And if he had known what aircraft they were—and in what state—he would have gone into the attack with a song in his heart.[3]

The Japanese air forces stationed in Indo-China and Formosa consisted of the 21st Flotilla under Admiral Tada and the 23rd under Admiral Takenaka. Between them they had one hundred and fifty ultra-modern Bettys, eighty-four twin-engined Sallys, one hundred and thirty-eight Kate dive-bombers, and a hundred and thirty-six Zeros, plus a rather mixed collection of reconnaissance and observation planes.

For the defence of the Philippines the American Army Air

---

[3] 'We were afraid of a preventive raid by the Americans, and as our attack, which was supposed to be synchronised with the attack on Pearl Harbor, could not take place at the time envisaged owing to bad weather, we were prepared for the worst. Imagine our surprise when we found the American planes, on Clark Field and elsewhere, lined up on the ground as if for a general inspection.' (Testimony by Admiral Tsukahara, September 1945.)

Force had five fighter-squadrons equipped with Curtiss P-40s, and there were also twenty-four old P-35s and twelve P-26s, of 1930 vintage, flown by Philippinos. At Nichols Field there was the 21st Squadron, at Iba Field the 3rd Squadron and at Clark Field the 20th Squadron, each with eighteen P-40s. At Del Carmen, the general maintenance centre, were the 17th and 34th Squadrons, which had received on 6th December, i.e. two days[4] before the attack, thirty-six P-40s.

The thirty-six P-40s were quickly assembled, and in the course of the process the armourers discovered that the firing contacts for the machine-guns just were not there. Improvised ones had to be made by a watchmaker in Manila. 'Prestone,' the cooling fluid for the engines, had also been left behind in the United States. San Francisco's reply was 'anti-freeze [sic] is not necessary in a climate like that of the Philippines.'

At 12.45 on 8th December two Japanese formations, one of thirty-four fighters and fifty bombers, the other of fifty-three fighters and fifty-four bombers, made a savage attack on the American airfields. Thirty-two Curtiss P-40s and twelve Flying Fortresses were destroyed in seven minutes—more than a third of the modern American aircraft available.

On the 10th the enemy attacked again, this time with one massive wave of a hundred bombers escorted by more than a hundred fighters. Twenty P-40s and fifteen P-35s took off to intercept them. The result was dramatic—only five American

---

[4] The international date line in the Pacific meant that 7th December at Pearl Harbor corresponded to 6th December in the Philippines.

fighters returned to base, all badly damaged; twenty-three Japanese planes had been damaged. General George, O/C 5th Interceptor Command, only had three modern planes left.

The next morning the Japanese landed in strength. Captains Bud Wagner, Sprague, Dyess and their comrades covered themselves with glory through nine days of desperate fighting. The P-40 showed itself to be absolutely outclassed by the Japanese Zero.

On 22nd December MacArthur, whose troops no longer had any air cover, decided to concentrate all his forces in the Bataan peninsula, to await reinforcements. It was an epic retreat, and by 24th December a proper defence line had been established and was being held.

It was also on 24th December that General George learnt, by a signal in code, that he ought to have received eighty-four P-40s and a hundred pilots from San Francisco. They had already left at the beginning of November, but were recalled through some administrative tangle between the Navy and Army Air Forces. With those reinforcements he could have smashed the Japanese landings.

'Too little, always too late!' Those disillusioned words were on every flying man's lips during the first two years of the war.

1st January 1942

5th Interceptor Command's control centre was reduced to one radar and telecommunications post which the Signal Corps had succeeded in setting up on the summit of Mount Mariveles. The aerials were slung on the topmost branches of the trees and a telephone line linked the post with General MacArthur's G.H.Q. in the tunnel of Corregidor fortress. Their SCR 297 transmitter was very powerful and could reach Del Monte, which was in communication with Australia. That was the only link these 800 men, lost in the jungle, had with the outside world.

To get the most out of his few remaining aircraft General George had scattered them on three tiny landing-strips hewn in the jungle. The best was a fairly straight section of the coast road at Mariveles. By a supreme stroke of luck large stocks of aviation spirit had been salved and hidden among the rocks. Even if the men starved, the twenty-odd Curtiss P-40s, the Americans' last hope, would be kept going. The men camped out where they could in the brush. There were twenty-three pilots, plus fitters, radio mechanics, armourers and all the staff personnel. All the M/T, with the exception of half a dozen trucks, had been abandoned.

The 24th Assault Group, comprising Squadrons 3, 17, 20, 21 and 34, had already lost forty-three pilots in aerial combat since 8th December and eighty-two P-40s, not to mention the poor P-35s of 21st Squadron massacred by the Zeros one after the other. The rest of the planes had been destroyed on the ground by bombing raids.

Ten fighters, plus two u/s ones for cannibalisation,[5] was in the end all that 24th Assault Group had with which to hold off a Japanese force of about six hundred planes in the sector. MacArthur had ordered the transfer of the other eight P-40s to the reserve at Mindoro, on the other side of the sea.

On 4th January, the day of the transfer, eighteen P-40s took off to intercept a raid by twenty-seven enemy bombers. The Bettys were faster than the Curtiss's with their engines worn out by three weeks of constant take-offs and dog-fights at full throttle.

The eight planes due for Mindoro soon gave up the useless pursuit and made for their new base. Only six got there—the other two vanished without trace, swallowed up by the sea or the jungle.

Unfortunately an enemy recce plane had seen the take-off that morning and had located two of the Americans' improvised landing-strips. As a result, Mariveles had to be abandoned on 5th January after a severe bombing raid. Bataan Field was now kept under observation twenty-four hours out of the twenty-four by relays of dive-bombers, which immediately shot up anything that moved on the strip. At dawn on the 6th, eighteen Zeros strafed the field and killed four men. It was time to move. Finally, round about midday, the four grounded P-40s managed to get into the air and catch three Kates by surprise and shoot them down. One of the Curtiss's crashed in flames during the fight but the three others got to Cabcaben.

Suddenly, in the night of 17th January, 2000 Japanese landed

---

[5] I.e. to be dismantled, and their individual parts made available for other planes.

at Agasin, in the rear of the Americans, right in the south of the peninsula. At 3 a.m.. by the light of truck headlights, the precious surviving P-40s were evacuated to Baguio, as the Japanese were approaching their objective, the airfield.

At Baguio, a small clearing in the thick jungle formed by a dried-up paddy field, George's men had managed to rough out a runway about 400 yards long and 35 wide. Carefully camouflaged shelters had been fashioned in the virgin forest and in the lee of rocks. And they did have six A.A. 75s and ten 13-mm. A.A. machine-guns.

In the night of the 19th, three Japanese destroyers landed 1500 more men. At dawn the P-40s tried to attack with pathetic 30-lb. anti-personnel bombs, but without doing much harm, as the enemy had already infiltrated into the jungle. When the planes came back the camp was under siege. The enemy had surrounded them on a perimeter of three miles. 5th Interceptor Command was irretrievably cut off.

The American Army, painfully defending itself in the north, was already short of men. 20,000 men, of whom 15,000 were Philippine Militia, stripped of everything, short of ammunition, with no artillery and no food, hemmed in against Mount Samat, were holding a line from Crion to Bagae against 100,000 crack Japanese troops, specialists in jungle warfare. The airmen could hope for no help from outside.

Every man took up arms, including the grounded pilots—staff, clerks, cooks, fitters, majors, colonels, everyone.

An old 300-h.p. Bellanca cabin passenger plane, flown by a heroic Philippine officer called Captain Jesus A. Villamor, did the dangerous trip to Mindanao every night, bringing back ammunition, submachine-guns, grenades and 45-calibre mortars in sections.

Then began a frightful ordeal which was to last until 12th February. Keeping the enemy out of mortar range of the airfield became a matter of life and death, otherwise the aircraft would be unable to take off. The battle in the jungle was joined. At the end of a fortnight the enemy had tightened his grip, and life became a nightmare. Less than fifty yards from the edge of the runway men were already lost, swallowed up by the jungle.

From the air the Philippine jungle is a solid mass of exuberant vegetation, as uniform as a pile carpet. But the plane only sees the serried tops of the trees, thrust up to the sky by the long smooth trunks, to which a mass of parasites cling. For men fighting in it, it is a degenerate putrefying plant-world, full of the stench of death. Daylight filters through an inextricable tangle of leaves, branches and creepers. When it reaches the ground it is only a sort of permanent watery twilight.

The Japanese were everywhere and nowhere. The dry crack of an automatic rifle, the shrill whistle of the tiny bullet, a hole in a leaf or in a forehead occasionally revealed the invisible enemy. The Americans built nests for themselves in the thickets with their hatchets, or scratched holes in the damp soil, and lay in them as in a coffin. On tenterhooks, they listened for the slightest noise, the least movement in the leaves—the first sign of the noiselessly rolling grenade or the quick bullet of the sniper in the trees. The hours passed slowly in that vitiated air, full of the stench of crushed toadstools and putrefaction, with never a breath of wind to give it life.

Water oozed through the soil and the hole soon became a cesspool. Soaked right through, teeth chattering with cold—and fever—men had to dig another foxhole further on and again expose themselves to the murderous bullets. A heavy silence till nightfall.

The shadows fell suddenly, without any transition, and it was always at the hour when the fireflies begin dancing that the Japanese attacked. Suddenly, somewhere, howls as of wild beasts, screams as of animals being slaughtered, shrill whistles, grenades going off. When the submachine-guns replied, the men in the other sectors anxiously peered into the night with blood-shot eyes, knowing that the Japanese attacked with bayonets and knives.

Was the defence perimeter holding? Three minutes, five, ten and it was all over for the time being. Only the shouts of the wounded and the moans of the dying broke the silence. The stretcher-bearers felt their way in the darkness. Then a brilliant red light showed through the trees and shots rang out again. The Japanese had set another of their diabolical booby-traps—they had dragged two or three wounded men out of their hiding-places on to a path, but without finishing them off. One of the medical orderlies had tripped over a wire, setting off a flare behind him, by the light of which the Japanese effortlessly picked off him and his companions.

When all had grown calm again, a soldier carried round the men's meagre rations from post to post. It was so pitch dark that he had to feel his way along a line of old telephone wire, a sort of Ariadne's thread, in order to find the advance posts through the maze of noxious undergrowth and trees.

At about 11 p.m. the fitters dragged two or three P-40s covered with branches out of their shelters and warmed up the engines. The pilots took off by the light of an improvised flare-path—cans full of sand soaked with petrol—and set off to shoot up the landing-craft in Manila Bay. This take-off was a miracle every time, as P-40s were not designed for night-flying. The fitters had knocked up exhaust-baffles of a sort out of bent bits of sheet metal, but that still further reduced the power of the tired engines. In addition, the food was so poor that the pilots' sight began to suffer, and night vision was the first thing to go.

Every take-off was an agonizing performance. Any plane deviating a few degrees from straight, or whose engine dropped a couple of hundred revs, immediately crashed into the trees. In two nights three planes were destroyed and two pilots killed. The third, Lieutenant Baker, was horribly burnt and could not be properly looked after with the resources at their disposal at Baguio. Captain Villamor took him off to Mindanao in his old Bellanca, but poor pain-maddened Baker took advantage of a moment when the pilot was not looking, opened the door and jumped into space.

In the night of 26th January General George decided to throw his seven remaining aircraft into a spectacular attack on Nichols and Nielsen Fields, now the Japs' main air-bases in the Philippines. The M.O. spent the afternoon examining the sixteen pilots one by one, to choose those in the best physical condition.

It was pitiful. They had on an average lost about forty-five pounds in weight and their blood pressure was so low that, according to the General's own final report, 'they ought even to be forbidden from climbing on the wing of a plane on the ground.' Their legs were devoured by leeches and covered with festering sores, and they all had dysentery so badly that half an hour in the air was absolute torture.

Finally Bud Wagner was chosen to lead the show, and Woolery, Stinson, Hall, Obert, Ibold and Brown were to go with him. The preparations were made in great haste. Two Jap planes, which took it in turns to keep a watch on Baguio, spotted the water-truck beginning to sprinkle the middle of the runway and destroyed it. That was serious, as it was going to be impossible to avoid raising a cloud of dust on take-off.

As it was essential to take the enemy by surprise, and as the Japs signalled any move of a plane to their anti-aircraft spotters on the coast by sending up multi-coloured rockets, everything had to happen fast.

A man stood by each can of the flare-path, ready to put a match to it the very second the engines started up. The moon shone in the sky, which would make the pilots' task a little easier.

At the given signal, a whistle-blast, a dozen flares lit up simultaneously, while the silence was shattered by the roar of the seven 1200-h.p. Allisons. No time for warming up the engines, as the aircraft had to be over the sea before the A.A. batteries had time to open up.

The first six P-40s succeeded in getting away in turn, but an impenetrable cloud of dust swirled up, worse after each take-off. The pilot of the seventh plane, completely blinded and unable to see the flare-path, swung drunkenly from side to side and did a ground-loop at a hundred miles an hour and turned a somersault. Three of the bombs under his wings exploded and the shattered fragments of the plane burst into flames. Badly burnt, his body riddled with splinters, Lieutenant Ibold was snatched from the flames by two of his mates, who rushed up, one of them being at once killed by a bullet going off in the blaze.

The characteristic whistle of the Curtiss formation faded in the night towards Corregidor.

The Japanese, who had by now completely written off the American Air Force, had taken no defensive precautions at all.

The lights of Manila stretched a dazzling chain round the bay, mirrored in a narrow luminous fringe on the still sea. The houses and barracks between Cavite and Calumpit were lit up and the pilots had no difficulty in getting their bearings. But Paranaque plain was covered by a patch of fog, as white as snow in the moonlight, and underneath were Nichols and Nielsen Fields!

Was there any clear space underneath? A difficult decision to make. Bud Wagner, taking the bold course, decided to attack Nichols with half his force, while the other three, led by Woolery, looked after Nielsen.

The Curtiss's came straight down through the mist, flying blind. The mist cleared a hundred feet from the ground.

The surprise was complete. A row of Bettys and Zeros in front of the control tower were machine-gunned—twenty-four planes left in flames. The N.C.O.s' Mess, lights blazing just as in peace-time, got sixteen direct hits from 60-lb. anti-personnel bombs, which created havoc inside. In one dormitory alone, thirty Japs were killed or wounded.

Same story at Nielsen Field. Thirteen enemy bombers destroyed.

The six Curtiss P-40s returned to base without a scratch. 'If we had had sixty instead of six P-40s, we might have altered the whole situation. Every night we angrily listened to senators or generals on the radio, promising the United States a production of 40,000 planes between now and the end of 1942. No doubt, but it didn't get us anywhere, we should have preferred four extra planes straight away. Always too late, always too late.'[6]

The Japs, shaken by the Manila show, attacked furiously for a whole week. One of their patrols got right through to the airstrip and threw two grenades on General George's tent, but in the end they were repulsed.

On 8th February, 24th Interceptor Command received orders to carry out a special daylight operation as requested by MacArthur. The Corregidor batteries wanted air photos of the area between Ternate and Cavite, to try and locate three heavy artillery pieces whose firing was getting dangerously accurate.

As they had no reconnaissance plane, they fixed a camera under the forward seat of an old training bi-plane, a Stearman PT-13. Mucking about over Cavite at 100 m.ph. and in broad

---

[6] Letter to the author from Colonel A. Ind, General George's Chief of Staff during the Bataan campaign, dated 7th October 1950.

daylight, without even a revolver, was plain suicide. Once again Captain Villamor heroically volunteered for the Job. A flight of six P-40s, led by Ben Brown, was going to try to keep the Zeros off him.

An hour after they had gone there was still no news, and all the men who were not actually on duty were collected round the General's tent, which had the loudspeaker tuned to the planes' wavelength.

The suspense was appalling. The General lay on his camp bed, struck down by a severe bout of malaria, and drops of sweat trickled down his pale, drawn face.

'Hullo, Leo to 9 MN, Leo to 9 MN, we are coming back.'

They were, but twelve Zeros had taken off beneath them. It was going to be a race to the death. Would the Stearman manage to land first? On top of that, the P-40s would literally have to protect its landing with their fuselages. They would thereby lose the advantage of altitude, without which P-40s were no match for Zeros.

There they were! Everyone rushed out on the strip. Villamor put his plane into a vicious side-slip which made the bracing-wires hum like the strings of a harp, then he levelled out between the trees, swish-tailed savagely and literally slammed his plane on the ground. Three of the six Curtiss's, in order to protect him right to the end, had put down their wheels and flaps, while the three others were circling round the strip at treetop level. Immediately afterwards the six Zeros came hurtling down.

But the Stearman had already been dragged into the lee of some rocks. The P-40s raised their flaps and their undercart.

Propellers at fine pitch, they desperately tried to get up to 3000 feet—the difference between life and death.

Carried away by their momentum, and over-estimating the speed of the Curtiss's, the Zeros misjudged their first attack and their firing was wide. The Jap fighters gained height and turned back on the P-40s, which had regrouped in pairs for mutual protection. The Curtiss's, hanging desperately on their propellers and practically stalling, were at the mercy of the fast, agile Zeros. As the latter separated, waggling their wings, to choose their individual victims, the six other Zeros came up from behind, in the sun. Taken by surprise, and mistaking the new arrivals for American reinforcements, the first Zeros broke away. It was a miracle, and Ben Wagner, an old hand at this game, seized his chance. Diving into the disordered group of Jap planes, the Curtiss's let fly with all they had and finally escaped into the clouds.

Two Zeros went into a spin, belching smoke, a third crashed in flames, and a fourth exploded, covering the airfield with burning fragments. The pilot's crumpled body fell between two shelters.

Just at that point the airfield's anti-aircraft defences opened up against the bewildered Japs. A Zero, framed by bursts, climbed towards the clouds and vanished into them. A few seconds later they heard the chatter of a Curtiss's machine-gun and then the crash of a collision—the interlocked remains of two planes floated down through the layer of strato-cumulus.

No parachute.

Ten minutes later the five surviving Curtiss's landed without mishap. The missing pilot was Lieutenant Earl R. Stone, Junior, who already had four confirmed successes to his credit.

On 12th February Baguio was liberated by the Japs' retreat southwards under pressure. The enemy who had infiltrated behind the American lines and were besieging Baguio were gradually pressed back towards Logaska Point.

The five P-40s were again based on the two coastal airfields, three at Bataan Field and two at Tacloban—where they survived twenty-six enemy air-raids in a fortnight.

The exhausted pilots were doing two trips a day—spotting for the artillery, dropping medical supplies to forward troops isolated in the jungle, strafing and bombing Japanese installations. They shot down seven Kate dive-bombers, but lost Lieutenant Hynes, brought down during a long dog-fight with five Zeros.

Only four P-40s were left, but the fitters at Mindoro succeeded in patching up two badly damaged ones which had been bombed and written off the previous December, and these unexpected reinforcements raised everybody's morale.

That very evening Woolery and Hall took off in the two reconditioned P-40s, whose practically new engines roused all the other pilots' envy. They intercepted for the first time 'Photo Joe,' a twin-engined Betty which turned up every day at the same time to take photos over Corregidor. The Betty, caught between them, tried to break loose. The two Curtiss's attacked simultaneously and the horrified spectators on the ground saw them both break up in the air at the first burst from their guns. Woolery and Hall were killed.

This tragedy profoundly affected all the flying personnel, and it was only the next day that the military police got to the bottom of the mystery. A pro-Japanese Sakdalist saboteur had been caught and he revealed under 'third degree' that the men in the San José group at Mindoro had received special instructions for sabotaging planes. It was only necessary to ram a few bullets forcibly up the barrels of the machine-guns with rods. This blocked them, and when the pilot fired the barrels burst, snapping the main spar and ripping open the wing, which disintegrated at once. The Sakdalists had done this to the two P-40s and the armourers at Tacloban had only had time to check on the actual loading of the machine-guns. The sabotage had therefore not been detected.

It was another very sad evening. The news from all the Allied fronts was getting more and more depressing—Benghazi retaken by Rommel, the *Repulse* and the *Prince of Wales* sunk off the Malayan coast. Every day the besieged Americans were more isolated.

On the 3rd March General George was called up at 11.30 by Palafox—the observation post on Mount Mariveles—on Red frequency, the one reserved for urgent messages in clear.

'Two large tankers, four troop-transports, including a ship of about 20,000 tons, are making for Subic Bay.'

It was the reinforcements the Japanese were waiting for to launch the final attack which should throw the Americans into the sea. Rather than bring them to Manila and then on by land, the enemy was bringing them direct to where they would be needed, at Olangapo, the harbour in Subic Bay.

The half-dozen American bombers remaining in the south-west Pacific were in Australia, being used by the Navy for long-range reconnaissance.

The Japanese ships were calmly approaching the coast, in broad daylight.

General George quickly made up his mind, and sent for Captain Dyess, commanding N. 21 Squadron. The tall, thin, gawky captain was the last survivor—with Bud Wagner, whom MacArthur had just sent back to Port Darwin—of the original eighty pilots the general had brought with him from the States just a year before.

In a few words the situation was explained to him. He must have his plane fitted with the bomb-rack which had been knocked-up by Sergeant Jack Day, the ace fitter at Tacloban. Now was the moment to put it into use. This gadget, made out of old valve-springs and motor-car pans, enabled a P-40 to carry a 500-pounder. But as there were only two of these bombs available, they had better not miss!

Dyess decided to make two trips, with one P-40 for close support and two more at 13,000 feet for top cover.

He took off, his plane vibrating and labouring with the extra load. Three minutes later the three escorting P-40s flew over H.Q. in impeccable formation, and disappeared behind Mount Mariveles, which bounded the horizon to the north-east with its gigantic crater.

From then on General George could only follow the progress of his aircraft from the radar operator's monotonous commentary.

'Here Prestone, Prestone, 9MN . . . distance 18, bearing 230—distance 19, bearing 225—distance 18.50, bearing 220.'

The planes must be climbing over the friendly area in a spiral.

'Distance 19.50, bearing 215—distance 22, bearing 216.'

Ah! They had set course on Subic Bay.

The sound of the engines had got lost in the booming of the Japanese guns firing away behind the mountain. The electric eye alone, cold and impersonal, kept track of the invisible planes on the screen of the SCR 228.

The three troop-transports were just edging into the jetty at Olangapo when the Curtiss's dived. Dyess's bomb grazed the hull of the biggest and exploded between the ship and the jetty, raising a mass of water which cataracted on to the decks. Developing a terrific impact off the immovable stone of the jetty, the shock wave stove in the ship's plates. She immediately took a heavy list. The decks were covered with helpless soldiers whom the P-40s now strafed furiously. Bunches of them jumped into the sea.

One of the tankers, trying to escape, was attacked in turn. The incendiary bullets perforated the tanks and petrol flooded out, swamping the alleyways. Suddenly the ship exploded in a volcano of flame. A sheet of fire with hundreds of soldiers swimming in it spread half a mile over the bay.

'Distance 14, bearing 225—distance 08, bearing 225 . . .'

The planes were coming back to reload.

The pilots were exultant. The second bomb was brought out, fused and man-handled into position under Dyess's aircraft by eight men using improvised levers.

The planes took off again. General George was both anxious—why no Zeros?—and elated, for the Navy observer on Mount Mariveles had just told him over the radio that through his telescope he had seen the 20,000-ton transport capsize with its human cargo still on board.

This time, Dyess decided he would go all out for a bull and release his bomb at point-blank range. He dived, struggling with the controls, to keep his plane in a straight line on the target. The airframe, too often repaired, started to show signs of breaking up and rivets on the wing surfaces began to spring loose.

Now! The bomb hit the *Nagura Mam* smack between its two red-and-white-banded funnels. The impact covered the sea all around with white foam and the ship took on a list and began to sink.

Now for a shoot-up! The four planes concerted their efforts and attacked a second tanker, but without any visible result this time. After two runs each, they left it and made for the other transport.

'Hullo Leo, Leo, here Prestone 9MN, look out! Enemy aircraft, distance 30, bearing 010. Look out!'

But it was too late. Before the Curtiss's could take up defensive formation or gain height the Zeros, alerted by the ships' SOS, fell on Olangapo like angry hornets.

This time there was little hope—one to ten, about. Lieutenant Fosse crashed in flames on the naval yards and Stinson dodged one Zero, only to crash into another. Dyess and Crellin battled on desperately. Their physical condition, after months of privation, was such that Dyess blacked out and vomited at each tight turn. They were irrevocably trapped low down over the water, the Zeros bearing down on them like an enraged pack of hounds.

Crellin's plane began to smoke. The pilot, choking, struggled to open the hood, but when it gave at last the air rushed in and the flames enveloped him. Dyess, now alone, kept up the desperate struggle. With each turn he succeeded in edging closer to Tacloban.

The unequal combat now continued over the base. Everyone had rushed out and was following the dog-fight, powerless to intervene. General George, completely unwrung, knelt down, with tears in his eyes and prayed aloud.

Dyess's Curtiss was now dragging a long white trail of smoke. It was immediately above the airfield, with the Zeros hot on its heels. Suddenly it flicked over on its back and the pilot jumped. The parachute opened out at tree level and the vegetation swallowed it up at once. George's prayers had been answered, for Dyess had jumped so low that the Japs did not have time to machine-gun him.

That was the end of 24th Interceptor Command. This last operation had accounted for the four last Curtiss P-40s at Bataan. On 9th April the very few survivors of the American Armed Forces in the peninsula capitulated. MacArthur had previously had Dyess transported to Mindoro in the old Bellanca, and he survived all his five 7.7-mm. bullet wounds to receive the Congressional Medal of Honour from President Roosevelt in person.

The Zero was for the Japanese what the Spitfire and the Messerschmitt 109 were for the British and the Germans.

Its proper name in the Imperial Japanese Navy was Mitsubishi A6M Type O; hence its nickname of Zero, given to it by the Americans. They meant nothing depreciatory by it: on the contrary.

It is easy to see why American flying and intelligence personnel soon found themselves having to give Japanese planes code names. It was impossible to sort out the fantastically complicated Japanese system of nomenclature, quite apart from the difficulties of pronunciation.

At the experimental stage each Japanese military plane was given an official 'Ki' number. This series was chronological from the blue-print stage and was common to all aircraft constructors. Later, when they were manufactured and distributed to squadrons, they got a registration which included the manufacturer's name, a number indicating the year of production in the Japanese calendar, a description of its functions in code and a type or sub-type number. To make things more complicated, the Japanese calendar was based on the year of the foundation of the Japanese Empire, 660 B.c.

Up till 1939 (i.e. year 2599 in Japan) the Navy and Army Air Forces used the last two figures to denote the type of aircraft. For example, they gave the designation of Type 99 both to what we knew as the Val dive-bomber and to the first version of the twin-engined Lily. After 1940 (year 2600) the Army used the number 100, and the Navy the 'O'. In subsequent years only the last figure was used.

It was all very complicated, especially as the same aircraft had two names if it was produced by two different factories. Even later, when the Japanese gave individual names to their military planes—names of constellations or meteorological phenomena—the difficulty remained because you never knew just what plane was being referred to, and it was impossible to pronounce the names in the Romagi phonetic transcription.

The Technical Air Intelligence Unit (T.A.I.U.) directed by Colonel MacCoy, whose task was the study of Japanese aeronautical material, decided to settle the problem once and for all. At that time—early 1942—all enemy aircraft were called Zero if they were fighters and Mitsubishi if they had more than one engine. It was an over-simplification, and dangerous when evaluating the potential strength of any given enemy airfield.

MacCoy hit on the idea of giving each Japanese plane an arbitrary name, usually an ordinary Christian name. In one month more than seventy-five names were allotted—Jake, Pete, Rufe, Zeke, etc. It could easily be deduced from the names chosen that the author came from Tennessee.

When MacCoy began to transmit the results of his labours to Washington he succeeded in completely jamming the radio services. MacArthur, C.-in-C. in the theatre of operations, who was at that time rather lukewarm about the air arm, blew up, thinking that the Air Force were communicating with the Pentagon in secret code behind his back. To reassure him

MacCoy christened the new Mitsubishi bomber Type 97 (Ki 21) 'Jane' after Mrs. MacArthur.

MacArthur allowed himself to be mollified, until one day he came across some of the 'poems' composed by airmen about the female personalities of the Jap planes. Like most service literary compositions, these were scarcely repeatable in polite company. A curt note from MacArthur led to 'Jane' being changed to 'Sally'.

As the supply of names began to run short, T.A.I.U. began baptising planes with the names of friends and relatives. Frank, Francis, Joe—the Christian names of Colonels MacCoy, Williams and Grattan, the top men in T.A.I.U.—were soon followed by Loise and June, MacCoy's wife and daughter.

When one realises that the Japanese produced no fewer than 118 different types of military aircraft in five years, it is easy to guess at the Chinese puzzle (if I may so describe it) which resulted, as only plain, short names would do, three syllables at the most, and not such as could be mistaken for something else over R/T. The Zero kept its name, which had already achieved wide popular recognition, in spite of its official appellation, 'Zeke'.

The Zero was a nasty surprise for the Americans. In 1941 they firmly believed that the Japanese only had absurd old monoplane fighters with fixed under-carriage, or bi-planes corresponding to their own obsolete 1930 planes. This belief was aided and abetted by the specialist periodicals and by the 'technical experts' of the press. Nobody dreamed that the Americans themselves would soon by only too happy to use their old Boeing P-26s with fixed undercarriage in the Philippines!

There is no point in enlarging here on the dangers of underestimating your enemy. Hitler did the same with the Russians' tanks and planes in 1941. (As history invariably repeats itself, the same imbecile attitude towards the Soviet post-war Air Force prevailed until the war in Korea.)

Naturally the awakening was rude and American pilots saw very quickly how far reality was from the official version. It was no use trying to take on a Zero in a dog-fight. It turned too tightly, climbed too fast and was generally as slippery as an eel.

The first pilot to learn this was Lieut. George Whiteman, on the occasion of the attack on Pearl Harbor, on 7th December 1941, and he paid with his life for a lesson which many of his comrades had to learn the hard way too. One after the other, Allied fighter-pilots got themselves shot down trying to find the correct tactics against that small, fast, agile gadfly. It was rather the same problem as the Luftwaffe's Messerschmitt 109 had with the handy and manoeuvrable Spitfire.

The Spitfire's reputation being what it was—and a thoroughly deserved one at that, since the Spit was a superb plane, and adored by those who flew it—the R.A.F. quickly sent out an Australian Spit Wing from England to Darwin.

This crack unit, equipped with Spitfire IXA's and commanded by the famous 'Killer' Caldwell, was composed entirely of experienced pilots who had been fighting the Luftwaffe for the past year, and it arrived in Australia complete with all its equipment, including a top-notch radar control system. The situation was critical, but the new wing, attributing the poor P-40 boys' pessimism to wounded pride, ignored their warnings and adopted a 'now we'll show 'em' attitude.

The answer was not long in coming. On 2nd May 1943 twenty-one Japanese bombers, escorted by thirty-two Zeros, raided Darwin. The interception, by thirty-two Spitfires, directed by an English radar controller, was superb. But after the battle, when the score was taken, there was no escaping the fact that thirteen Spitfires had been lost for one bomber and five Zeros destroyed. The Australian fighter-pilots' enthusiasm was a shade dampened.

On 30th June twenty-seven Bettys escorted by thirty Zeros came back for more. Once again the Australians intercepted impeccably, but for eight bombers and two Zeros, six Spitfires out of the forty-one which took off never came back. The Australians were beginning to catch on, for this time they had avoided the fighters as far as possible and concentrated on the bombers.

In spite of all their experience, the greatest Allied aces always got caught out in the end—and in aerial combat your first mistake is usually your last. The great Tommy MacGuire—the acknowledged ace in the Pacific after Bong's departure—with his thirty-eight successes, including twenty-one Zeros, went the same way as the others.

On 7th December 1944, exactly three years after Whiteman's death, MacGuire was leading a patrol of four P-38 Lightnings in a roving mission against the enemy airfields at Cebu and Los Negros. His No. 2 was Mayor Rittmayer, fourteen successes. Two thousand feet above Los Negros they saw a beautiful shining black Zero threading his way through the mountains. This plane, as was learnt the next day, had just been strafing an American torpedo-boat which was searching for a pilot ditched in the sea, and he was probably on his way home, short of ammunition.

The four Lightnings dived. The Zero patiently waited until they were within range. Then he did a tight left turn which brought him on Rittmayer's tail. One well-aimed burst and one of Rittmayer's engines caught fire. Surprised, he called for help and MacGuire came up. The Zero now did a tight right turn, fired again, and MacGuire crashed in flames. A loop, a final burst, and the remains of Rittmayer's plane were scattered over the enemy airfield. Having exhausted his ammunition, the Zero calmly went on turning inside the other two Lightnings, who could not get at him. They had to remove themselves at full throttle only too thankful to be still in one piece, when six other Zeros took off to join in. Thank goodness all Jap pilots were not of the same calibre as this one.

One of the pilots who flew Tempests with me in 1945, an incredible Australian called Bay Adams (see *The Big Show),* told me about his first scrap with Zeros on 6th July 1943.

He was one of a formation of twenty-four Spitfires which intercepted the regular bi-weekly raid by twenty-seven bombers and twenty-one Zeros. Following instructions, they immediately dived on the bombers, ten of which were shot down without loss, the remainder jettisoning their bombs. Having completed their task, the Spitfires tried to fade away, but the Zeros reacted very aggressively and there was nothing for it but to face them.

Bay, who had just pulverised a Sally, was rash enough to chase after a Zero who was doing a shallow dive. Just as the Spitfire opened fire at 300 m.p.h. the Zero did a perfect loop of 200 yards radius, which brought him on the Spitfire's tail. Bay, flabbergasted, by sheer reflex action luckily flicked over on his back and got away by a vertical dive, from 23,000 feet to practically sea-level. On that day seven Spitfires were shot down, and only two Zeros could be added to the score.

These few examples show that the Zero was a very worthy opponent, in the hands of quite average pilots. What was the Japanese designers' secret?

Colonel Hayward, from the test centre at Wright Field, has given the answer in one sentence: 'The Zero?—it's a light sports plane with a 1300-h.p. engine!' And it is true that the unladen weight of the Zero was under 4000 lb., while the Spitfire IX, same size and with an only slightly more powerful engine, weighed 6500 lb. Yet both had the same main armament, two 20-mm. cannon, and carried much the same number of shells.

The Zero, 1942 version, climbed to 10,000 feet in three minutes dead, and at the absolutely phenomenal angle of 45 degrees, while the two standard 1944 American fighters, the P-47G and the P-38G, took four minutes to reach the same height. At 23,000 feet the Mustang P-51, the fastest U.S. Army fighter in 1944, only had a margin of 65 m.p.h. over the 1942 Zero. But in 1944 the Zero had been replaced in the front line by the George, which batted along perfectly happily at 425 m.p.h.

The real secret of the Zero lay in the method of construction. Instead of being built in separate units—wings, fuselage, tail-unit, engine-housing, engine, etc.—and assembled afterwards, the Zero was constructed all of a piece, or, rather, two pieces. The engine, cockpit and fore part of the fuselage combined with the wings to form one rigid unit. The second unit consisted of the rear part of the fuselage and the tail. The two units were fixed together by a ring of eighty bolts.

All our engineers will tell you that from the point of view of rational construction this was fantastic. Perhaps, but the fact remains that a single factory at Nagoya turned out 7000 Zeros in three years.

The saving in weight was in the region of 45 per cent, and yet the structure was very strong. Special light alloys—in whose manufacture the Japanese were past masters—were used to the extreme limit of stress.

The engine was the 14-cylinder radial Nakajima Sakae—a development of our good old Gnome-Rhône K-14, which deepens the impression that we French were the only ones who could not get the best out of our own designs. It was stepped up from 1020 to 1315 h.p. at take-off between 1940 and 1943. By then it had a two-stage supercharger, an inverted flying carburettor and a three-bladed Mitsubishi-Hamilton propeller with a diameter of 10 feet 6 inches. With this last engine the Zero reached 340 m.p.h. at 20,000 feet altitude, computed from tests on Wright Field on a Zero captured in reasonably good condition. And this one, it must not be forgotten, was a carrier-borne plane, with the consequent handicaps of landing-hook, water-tight compartments in the wings and so forth.

On the other hand, the construction of a fighter plane being essentially a compromise, the Zero had one grave weakness. The Japanese designers had only an attacking plane in view and no thought was given to defence. The German designers of 1939 thought on much the same lines and they were to pay dearly for it.

The idea behind the Zero was that it would sweep away all opposition before the enemy had time to hit back. It had no self-sealing tanks, no armour-plating for the pilot. It was a death-trap. While the heavier Allied aircraft could sustain tremendous damage and still preserve the pilot's precious life, the Zero, although it stood up to the tightest and most violent aerobatics—it withstood up to 12 g[7]—crumpled up when hit, its petrol tanks burst into flames and it literally tore to pieces in the air like tissue paper.

The correct combat technique against such a plane was to keep out of range and fight on the dive and the climb, avoiding horizontal turns. (The Focke-Wulfs used the same tactics against us when we had Spitfires, but the British fighter's speed enabled it to hold its own.) Once the Allied fighter-pilot had assimilated this, assuming that he was still alive, he could convert his plane's greater weight into speed and, resisting the temptation of trying to out-turn the enemy, end up by getting him in the sights. A single burst of 20- or 13-mm. was then enough.

The general characteristics of the Zero were very orthodox. A wing-span of 34 feet, a length of 30 feet. A comfortable wing area of 235 square feet gave it a loading of a mere 20 lb. to the square foot, compared with the 55 lb. of my Tempest. The workmanship was very sound, and the cockpit was comfortable, though rather a tight squeeze for the normal European pilot. The instruments were well laid out and within easy reach. The accessories were of good quality and for the most part American, manufactured under licence. The only exceptions were the petrol gauges, which

---

[7] g=centrifugal force, measured in multiples of the force of gravity.

were unreliable—very unpleasant for pilots who did nearly all their flying over the sea—and the hydraulic system, which constantly developed leaks.

The armament comprised two 20-mm. Oerlikon cannon, light model, in the wings with 100 shells each, and two 7.7-mm. machine-guns firing through the propeller with 600 rounds each. Under the wings were permanent racks for either two 60-kilo phosphorus bombs with barometric fuses for aerial attacks on Super-fortress formations, or two 'fixed' 250-kilo bombs for Kamikaze missions. In the latter case it was obviously impossible to indulge in manoeuvres involving negative g.

The Zero had three internal tanks with a capacity of 150 gallons, plus a drop-tank—it was the first fighter in the world to be so equipped—with a capacity of 100 gallons, slung between the two legs of the undercarriage. With these it had a radius of action of about 300 miles, a useful one for the time.

A special model of the Zero was built for the Japanese Army. To increase its lateral manoeuvrability the wings were clipped, rather like the Spitfire V-D. Its first code-name was Hap, after General Henry 'Hap to his friends' Arnold, C.-in-C. of the American Air Force, but not for long. It appears that at a Staff meeting in Washington an officer was describing the battle of Leyte, explaining to a group of delighted generals that large numbers of Haps had been brought down in flames. Arnold went up in smoke and demanded to know who had thought up the name. The officer, not knowing quite what to say, lamely said that the name was being changed and, without even knowing whether Arnold really was annoyed, sent an urgent signal to

T.A.I.U. So Hap became Hamp, but two years later, when the, armistice came, T.A.I.U. were still rocking with laughter.

CHAPTER THREE

A DAY IN MALTA

1942

'WHEN I wrote in my diary: "Odd sort of war, and odd sort of way of starting it," I had in mind all that immense waste of money, equipment and human lives, all that chaos of haste and confusion.

If we had prepared for the war in time, the cost would have been a drop of water instead of the ocean. And then we in the Services, with only the pittance they deigned to give us to defend our country with, we fail, and the politicians want our heads on a charger, because they have to find scapegoats.'

Air Marshal SIR HUGH LLOYD
A.O.C. Malta in 1941

'I hope the lessons of Malta will not be forgotten. I trust that never again shall our unpreparedness lead to our men having to face such odds or be stretched so near to the ultimate limit of endurance.'

Marshal of the Royal Air Force Lord Tedder
Chief of Air Staff

* * *

A Day in Malta

I met S/Ldr. George Beurling, D.S.O., D.F.C., D.F.M. and Bar, for the first time at Catfoss at the end of July 1944.

I had finished my tour of operations on 7th July with escort flights over the Normandy landing. Catfoss was the advanced gunnery school where the R.A.F. collected pilots who were experienced and successful, to try and evolve and perfect new shooting and fighting techniques and new weapons and sights.

I had arrived that morning with a group of other pilots drawn from all the corners of the earth where fighting was going on. After dumping my kit in the room allotted to me, I went over to the Officers' Mess for lunch.

In one corner of the empty anteroom, slouched, or rather draped over an arm-chair, there was a type in battle-dress with no badge of rank and no ribbons, and with an old pair of ladies' stockings wound round his neck. To my rather embarrassed greeting—I was wondering what the hell this bloody erk was doing here—he responded with a vague grunt.

I buried myself in the latest number of *Punch* and then, tired after my journey, I went fast asleep. I was soon awakened.

'Who are you? Stand up! What the bloody hell are you doing here?'

It was a newcomer, also in battle-dress, but whose badges of rank were hidden by an Irvine jacket. I only saw his back view and did not at first recognise his parade-ground voice. Without shifting his position in the least, but merely raising his head, my friend the erk answered with two short pithy syllables. The man in the Irvine jacket absolutely exploded, and this time I recognised him as Group Captain 'Sailor' Malan, D.S.O., D.F.C.—thirty-two enemy aircraft to his credit—who was in command at Biggin Hill when I was a sergeant-pilot in the 'Alsace' squadron, and who must now be the Big White Chief here at Catfoss.

'Get out of here and come back when you're properly dressed.'

There was no mistaking the note of command in the angry voice. This time the Canadian realised who was the boss and, with an exasperatingly insolent leer, he got up in a leisurely way, picked up a battered oil-stained cap with a ragged peak from under his arm-chair and sauntered out of the room. I had got up too and Malan turned round and recognised me. He came over and shook hands.

'Hullo, Clostermann, glad to see you again. Do you know who that was? Beurling, you know, the Malta type. I soon saw what his little game was. He was just waiting for some sprog P/O to tick him off so that he could tell him where he got off. He's been doing that every morning for a week in the waiting-rooms at Air Ministry. But this time he picked the wrong bloke. I was shooting Jerries down when he was still in nappies. Anyway, it was a good lesson for him, and it's better it should have happened on the first day, in private. He'll know now that he's got to behave himself here. But don't get him wrong, he really is a remarkable type.'

I soon saw why Malan wanted it understood straight away that he was going to stand no nonsense. His crowd at Catfoss were an extraordinary bunch of crack fighter-pilots of all nations: Kingaby, D.S.O., D.F.M. and two Bars, who had brought down eighteen Messerschmitt 109s in three months over London; 'Timber' Woods, D.S.O., D.F.C., from Malta; Jack Charles from Biggin Hill; two Czech night-fighter pilots with twenty-five successes between them; the Pole, Salsky, D.S.O., D.F.C. and two Bars; and some Americans, including the famous Richard Bong from the Pacific. I felt pretty small beer in this company with my mere D.F.C.

Bong and Beurling stood out very sharply from the rest. The Englishmen, and also the foreigners who had been trained by the R.A.F., were usually modest and unwilling to talk about themselves. Above all they had a horror of 'line-shooting'.

Bong, who at that time had thirty-seven successes against the Japs in his Lockheed Lightning, had arrived from the States a week before with the firm intention of showing those poor R.A.F. boys how to shoot down enemy planes.

Bong and Beurling soon became inseparable; it was inevitable. They were both outstanding shots, remarkable flyers, and they both had an excellent opinion of themselves. I know that fighter-pilots are given to that, but they certainly were extreme cases. With Beurling it was just youthful high spirits, and also the result of the incredible difficulties he had had to surmount to become a pilot at all. With Bong it was simply congenital.

As birds of a feather flock together, I soon made up the trio. Jacques Remlinger, who arrived a few days later, added himself to the group, and we were soon known as the 'Catfoss Quads'. Our unvarying talk of planes, cannon, shooting and tactics and our long stories of what we had done, illustrated by much waving of the arms, quickly created a vacuum round us. I kept notes of our talk, and they are full of valuable gen about Malta and the Pacific.

Bong was killed at the beginning of 1945 while on a training flight in a Shooting Star, after he had got three more scalps in the Pacific. He was the only Allied pilot—with the possible exception of 'Killer' Caldwell, the Australian—to have brought down forty enemy planes for certain.

Beurling, 'Screwball' to his friends, crashed in 1947 as he was taking off from Rome with an old American war-surplus plane crammed with ammunition for Israel during the war in Palestine. Poor George, he had an organic craving for danger and excitement and he had been unable to re-adapt himself to civilian life.

* * *

Beurling, like a number of other R.A.F. pilots, had volunteered for service in Malta. All those who were due to go out there called Malta 'the fighter-pilot's paradise'. As very few of those who went ever lived to tell the tale, the name stuck.

Malta, a small island with an area of about 90 square miles, isolated by the fall of France in 1940 and the lack of vision of the military chiefs in North Africa, was a painful thorn in the flesh of the Axis powers. That thorn produced a malignant abscess and the Afrika Korps, in spite of the genius of Rommel, died of it.

The importance of Malta as a strategic base lay in its capacity for offensive action, lying as it did half-way between Africa and Italy. Its strength in numbers of aircraft was always tiny, but its twenty-odd Blenheim and Beaufort torpedo-bombers, eight Glenn Martin Baltimores and thirty Wellington night-bombers, scattered on the six miles of runway at Luqa and Safi or hidden in underground shelters, played the major part in strangling the supply route to the Germans in Libya.

These few planes, flown by brave and determined crews, and suffering 30 per cent losses per trip, were constantly replaced; they succeeded in seven months of 1941 in sinking 56 per cent of the merchant tonnage available to the Germans and Italians in the Mediterranean.

In June 1941, 34,000 tons were sunk, 25,000 tons severely damaged and to all intents and purposes put out of action, 27,500 tons damaged. For July the figures were 83,000, 64,000 and 37,000; for August 122,900, 28,800 and 25,200.

Ciano wrote in his diary at this time: 'This Rommel campaign is becoming sheer madness. Our merchant fleet will not last a year at this rate.'

In the Proceedings of the Fuhrer's Naval Conferences, translated by the Admiralty, Doenitz admits on page 1231 (September 1941): 'Even with all the Spanish tonnage and the ships we could seize if we invaded Southern France, even by increasing construction tenfold in Italian shipyards, we could not keep up another Rommel campaign for one year. Malta must be destroyed.'

On page 1412 the Reich Commissioner for the Merchant Navy says (9th November 1942): 'Marshal Rommel has informed me of the havoc and confusion caused among merchant shipping by the planes from Malta.'

At about this time Rommel wrote to Hitler: 'I have personally warned Marshal Kesselring of the tragic consequences for my lines of communication between Italy and Africa if he does not succeed in establishing air superiority over Malta.'

The Germans and Italians certainly tried. For two years Malta was plastered with bombs. Two Fliegerkorps—i.e. 600 Junkers 88s and Messerschmitt 109s—were kept massed under Kesselring in Sicily, hardly eighty miles away. Malta became a death-trap. For 'the 300,000 prisoners', as the German radio used to call them, there was no refuge. Even London could at a pinch have been evacuated elsewhere.

Relations between Rommel and Kesselring got more and more strained. Rommel hoped Malta would be pulverised within three months, and at the beginning of 1942 he was fuming at the non-arrival of his 600 planes immobilised in Sicily. They would have turned the scale in Libya.

Malta, starving, with little petrol or supplies, with A.A. gun barrels worn smooth, could put in the air to defend itself an average of twelve to eighteen Spitfires in the morning. By 6 p.m. this number was generally down to four. Often, for two days on end, Malta only had five Spitfires airworthy.

The Germans never succeeded, in spite of desperate efforts, in preventing the torpedo-planes from operating. They were never in a position to launch a landing operation like the one on Crete, although there were only seventy-five miles to cross and the garrison consisted of a mere 14,000 badly armed troops.

What do the French chiefs in North Africa think now as they try to explain away their inaction by arguments about a hypothetical German landing?

On the other hand, it was possible to bring supplies into Malta only in dribs and drabs, by air. Every attempt to get a naval convoy through to the beleaguered island ended in heavy losses.

Takali airfield alone, in April 1942, got thirty-two times the weight of bombs that fell on Coventry.

Aircraft maintenance—there are very nearly half a million components in a Spitfire—was a perpetual problem. If a 20-mm. shell made a hole in the wing of one of the remaining aircraft it was a major calamity. The fitters worked day and night, in appalling conditions. The pilots, worn out, and all a prey to 'Malta dog', a kind of acute dysentery brought on by eating the island's vegetables, had to do up to five trips a day.

Luckily, as in the Battle of Britain, the radar warning system and cast-iron discipline of the squadrons enabled the few available aircraft to be put to the maximum use.

Kesselring later said: 'I have never been able to understand how and where the R.A.F. on Malta managed to hide its eight or ten Spitfire squadrons.' Eight or ten! What would have happened had he known there was only one squadron of Hurricanes and two of Spitfires, with on an average only 15 per cent of their planes serviceable?

As fighter reinforcements could not be flown in direct because the planes' range was too short, they had to be brought on aircraft-carriers to within 120 miles of the island. In these operations Britain lost the carrier *Eagle*, sunk by a submarine on her third trip, and the *Illustrious*, which was so badly damaged on her fourth trip that she had to be sent in convoy to the United States for refitting. The American carrier *Wasp* later did the trip three times, but then gave up. At that time aircraft-carriers in the Pacific were invaluable.

When the Battle of Malta ended in victory on 1st January 1943, it had cost 844 Spitfires and the lives of 518 R.A.F. pilots. Kesselring had lost 390 Junkers 88s, 403 Messerschmitt 109s and 104 Junkers 87s. The Italian contribution to the total score was 237 Macchi 202s, 333 Cant Alcyones and S.M.79s, plus an assortment of other types ranging from the Caproni Reggiane 2001 to three-engined flying-boats.

It was in mid-1942, when Kesselring and the Regia Aeronautica d'Italia were making their last desperate effort, when Malta's fate—and therefore the Mediterranean's—was hanging on a thread, that 'Screwball' Beurling appeared on the scene.

* * *

Malta, 'the fighter's paradise,' 9th June 1942

The *Eagle*, escorted by two destroyers, pressed ahead and left behind the British convoy bound for Malta. It was 5 a.m., just before sunrise. The carrier's deck was covered with Spitfire Vs equipped with auxiliary tanks.

The pilots gave their planes a final check over. They were Spit V-Cs ('tropical') armed with four 20-mm. cannon. They were at least brand-new planes, and at a time when everyone, from

Moscow, to London, from Australia to Alaska, from Libya to the Caribbean, was screaming for fighters, the pilots felt they had not done too badly to get them.

All the same, they were slightly nervous—not one of them had ever taken off from a carrier. While they strapped themselves in, the fitters finished stowing their meagre possessions in the magazines of the machine-guns and of two of the cannon—the other two cannon were loaded. Over the Tannoy came the naval flight-officer's final instructions: navigation gen, courses, E.T.A.s frequencies, etc.

At 6.05 a.m. the first Spitfire took off. Pointing his yellow flag, the deck officer signalled Beurling to get under way. This was it. Rather tensed, he slowly opened the throttle while keeping the brakes hard on. As soon as the tail lifted and the Spit began to champ at the bit, he let her go. Drawn by its 1500-h.p. engine, and with a 30-m.p.h. head-wind and the ship's own 20 knots helping, the plane was airborne almost immediately.

By 6.30 the last Spit had taken off and the *Eagle* immediately turned about. The Algerian coast was only thirty miles away, and there might be enemy submarines lurking around. Already in formation, the thirty-two planes receded in the distance, heading east on their flight to Malta.

The sea was blue, without a wrinkle. To the right was the violet line of the Tunisian coast, down below the white patch formed by the island of Lampedusa, over there to the left at the foot of that thundercloud forming was Sicily, with its fourteen airfields crammed with Messerschmitts.

More and more frequently, as Malta drew nearer, snatches of

conversation came over the R/T. Interference from German radio-location also began to jingle in the pilots' ears like an antique telephone bell.

The formation was flying at 24,000 feet and the cold was intense in spite of the sun. Fifteen minutes to go. Malta called:

'Hullo, Condor leader, this is Timber calling. Steer 081 and get a move on. Do not answer. Repeat, do not answer. Out.'

Things must be hotting up, and Woodhall, the controller, was getting anxious. He had no doubt seen on his radar screen an enemy raid forming over Sicily. It was probably going to develop into a race, if the Luftwaffe were not to catch them with their pants down as they landed, for the Germans had cathode-ray tubes too.

Malta ahead! A big grey and green oval, perched on white cliffs resting on the sea, and flanked to the north-west by two small islands of Comino and Gozo.

The formation split up into sections of four, diving separately. Details became discernible—the seething bay of Marsa Xlokh, the deep gash of Valetta harbour, ringed by tiers of flat-roofed houses, the web of hedges and stone walls cutting up the arid fields. Further on, the leprous sore of the main airfield, riddled with bomb craters.

Beurling had pushed back his hood and, while the first sections, with their flaps and undercarts down, were joining the circuit, he had a good look round.

Accustomed to the orderly arrangement of English airfields, he was taken aback at the sight of this stretch of ground, five miles long, with bits of runway everywhere and sinuous tracks disappearing into underground shelters. This extraordinary airfield was really three—Luqa, Safi and Hal Far—connected by two gravel strips, so that in effect a plane could take off or land anywhere, i.e. on whichever the last enemy raid had left intact.

However serious the damage, there was always some serviceable corner left. Enormous heaps of stones were dotted here and there, for filling in the new craters as soon as the raid was over. All round the perimeter, except where it ran along the cliff, there was a series of bays with thick walls, to protect parked planes from splinters. Remains of burnt-out wings and fuselages were scattered about everywhere.

Six Spitfires took off to cover the newcomers' landing. The field was swarming with men. Beurling did not quite know where to land. In the end he just followed the others down and found himself on a bumpy track at the end of which stood a group of soldiers waving him on. As he came past, two of them grabbed hold of his wing-tips while a third jumped on the wing and caught hold of his shoulder. Through the wind from the propeller this one yelled into his ear that he had better hurry up, Jerry was on the way.

In the end he found himself in a kind of rabbit burrow formed by heaps of petrol cans filled with sand. Before he had time to draw breath he was surrounded by a gesticulating crowd of extraordinary-looking individuals, unshaven and dressed in relics of the uniforms of all three Services. The fitter who had guided him in switched his engine off. Three muscular types grabbed the tail and swung the plane round so that it faced the airfield again. More men came staggering up with cans of petrol.

Beurling, flabbergasted, was ejected from his seat by a pilot who promptly took his place. Trying to keep out of the way of all these madmen he found himself in a slit trench at the back of the burrow. All his goods and chattels, lovingly stowed away in the wings, were sent flying in every direction.

'Get a move on, get a move on!' Everybody seemed to be shouting the same thing. The armourers came up at the double, screw-drivers between their teeth and festooned with belts of shells and cartridges. The radio-fitter had already clapped on his ear-phones, opened the fuselage panels, changed the crystals in the set and checked the battery terminals. The empty oxygen bottle was changed for a full one, which was ready waiting in a corner.

The pilot was getting impatient and drumming on the fuse-lage. Beurling, not quite knowing what to do, mechanically lit a cigarette. It was immediately snatched out of his mouth by a type who, before he had time to protest, bawled something at him and rushed back to his job. He might have known better; petrol was being brought up by a chain of soldiers and poured in the open through a large lined funnel.

The auxiliary tank was whisked off the plane.

'Hurry up, for Christ's sake!'

Already in the distance they could hear the Bofors batteries opening up. Bang, bang, bang, bang, bang—the five barks from one charger—bang! bang! bang! bang! bang! The Jerries must have arrived.

The ground-crew worked on frantically. From all over the field came the roar of Merlin engines starting up.

'O.K.? Contact!'

The men sprang off the Spitfire as it too started up, raising a furious wind which picked up Beurling's trampled shirts and underclothes and flung them into the air.

The pilot took the aircraft out of the bay with savage bursts of throttle which made the rudder vibrate. Still flat on one wing was an armourer, hanging on to the leading edge with one hand while he screwed down the last machine-gun panel with the other. Just as the Spit opened up to take off, he let go everything and rolled on to the ground, only just escaping being bashed in by the tail-plane.

Beurling was now alone. The crowd of madmen had vanished into thin air. He emerged from his hole and made for the open. He ran into three other pilots from the *Eagle*, just as dazed as himself, who dragged him along in a frantic rush for a shelter. It was high time. The air vibrated with the powerful rumbling roar of a big formation very high up, and the shriller sound of Spitfires attacking. The staccato crackle of the machine-guns stood out above the muffled boom-boom-boom of the 20-mm. Hispano cannon.

Look out! He just had time to turn round and see six Messerschmitt 109s, which had sneaked in low over the water, jump Hal Far cliff and streak across the field at 400 m.p.h. with all guns blazing.

It was Beurling's first glimpse of a 109. In France, when he was on 222 Squadron, he had met only Focke-Wulf 190s.

One of the 109s passed within ten yards of him, and the deafening roar of his engine mingled with the whine of the 40-

mm. shells from the A.A., firing horizontally and spraying the ground with splinters.

Just at that moment Beurling was sent flying head first into a trench by a push from one of his mates. He raised his head. The Junkers 88s—about fifty of them, escorted by sixty Messerschmitt 109s—were starting their dive. They were peeling off one by one and coming down in a 65-degree dive on the airfield in one unbroken line. The deep tone of the engines had changed to a screaming crescendo. The earth quivered, and sand trickled into the trenches. Bombs ripped down with a noise like an express train. The 88s flattened out at 1500 feet, their glasshouse noses and their elongated nacelles clearly visible.

The bombs exploded with a terrifying crump, great clods of earth flew up, splinters whizzed murderously, mowing down everything in their path. Each explosion sent a shock wave through the earth and each time Beurling felt a thump like a kick in the stomach.

The empty cases of the 20-mm. fell like hail, clanging against the empty cans. A Junkers 88, hit, continued its dive and crashed with a tremendous roar between two parked Wellingtons, which immediately burst into flame. Clouds of dust rose, mixed with smoke. The air stank of hot metal, sulphur and cordite. Shell splinters rained down.

A muffled explosion, followed by two others—another Junkers 88 had crashed, the wreck bouncing along in a sheet of flame.

Four parachutes hung above, stupidly silent amidst the infernal din.

A minute's relative calm on the ground while the battle raged 10,000 feet up. Planes circled in pairs, pursuer and pursued; wings glinted in the sun, and all the time the rattle of machine-guns went on. Now and then a plane broke away from the mêlée, trailing white smoke—over there, a Spitfire, and that ball of fire plummeting into the sea was a Messerschmitt 109.

The sky was thick with black clusters of A.A. bursts—like lumps of coal thrown up by the Bofors batteries.

A new wave of bombers came cascading down. Two Junkers 88s, harried by Spitfires and both with engines on fire, broke from the line and dived towards the sea.

Very high in the sky, well above all the turmoil, five little bright dots could be seen in impeccable formation. They were five Italian Cants. Nobody took any notice of them, but their perfectly grouped stick of bombs fell plumb on the intersection of the two runways on Safi airfield. How those bombs managed to fall through all those whirling planes without smashing a single one was a miracle.

The newly arrived pilots, covered with dust and rubble, shaken by the exploding bombs, huddling down to avoid the hail of stones and splinters, were rocked to their foundations. This really was war!

Ten minutes later it was all over. The Spitfires, fuel running low and ammunition spent, came into the circuit to land. Five Hurricanes from Takali airfield at the other end of the island flew above Luqa to protect the landing and the hurried dispersal of the planes. Beurling went back to his rabbit burrow to look for his belongings and wait for his plane to come back. He failed to find his razor or his toothbrush, which must have been left behind somewhere in the wings.

The planes were now coming in. Two with damaged under-carts had to belly-land, while a third with a good square yard of wing missing did a ground loop and turned arse over tit. Just about one plane in three was obviously damaged in one way or another. A promising look-out!

A pilot who came past, exhausted and eyes bloodshot, and humping his parachute, called across:

'No point waiting for your Spit. Norman Lee was flying it and he got the chop. Get weaving, or you'll miss the Mess bus, and it's a five-mile walk!'

The Mess was an old chalk quarry, a smoky tunnel, a hundred yards long and emerging straight into a coast road. The roof was pierced with ventilation shafts, but in the daytime there was insufficient current to work the fans; what there was of it was reserved for the dim bulbs and the water pumps. The air was heavy with the smell of sweat, cooking and tobacco smoke.

About a hundred and fifty N.C.Os. from the fighter and torpedo-bomber squadrons slept and ate there all crowded to-gether. The officers were no better off. Their billets had been bombed three times and they lived in a kind of gipsy encamp-ment composed of tarpaulins and corrugated-iron sheets stretched over remains of walls. You roasted in summer and froze in winter. No one was worrying overmuch about the winter at this time as the question was rather whether Malta would hold out even till autumn.

Lunch consisted of five shrivelled olives, one slice of fried corned beef, four ounces of bread, three semi-ripe dried figs and a cup of tea. Pilots also had a right to two tablespoonfuls of raw shredded carrots soaked in cod-liver oil, for the essential vitamins, and a sulphur pill against diarrhoea.

Beurling was still too shaken by his eventful arrival to have any appetite. In addition, the pervading stink of petrol and oil smoke made his gorge rise. As there was no coal, the cookers were fed on old sump-oil—a damaged aircraft was a godsend, as it meant hot soup for two or three days.

Poor Screwball! Scarcely six hours before, he had been getting outside a comfortable breakfast with all the trimmings at a large waxed-oak table in the aircraft-carrier's air-conditioned mess— an absolute pleasure-cruise! Now he was in a different world altogether. The fighter-pilot's paradise! With all those Junkers 88s and Messerschmitt 109s spoiling for a fight it was possibly a paradise up in the air. But a paradise on earth, no!

He went and sat on a rickety chair with Hesslyn, a New Zealander, Buchanan, a South African, Gil Gilbert, Billy the Kid and a few others of his crowd. The contrast was striking between the clean-shaven unlined faces of the new arrivals from the *Eagle* in their new Gibraltar-issue battle-dress, and the stubby faces—not a Gillette blade on the island—soiled shirts and tattered denims of the others.

'When Tedder passed this way a month ago,' said Mickey Butler, a Malta pilot of four months' standing who had already acquired seven confirmed successes, a D.F.M. and dysentery, 'we shook him rigid; I thought he was going to get out his wallet and give us ten bob each to buy a new shirt.'

1520 hours

'Screwball' was already on 'immediate readiness' and sat strapped in his cockpit. The twelve Spitfires of 249 Squadron were lined up at the end of the runway, ready to take off at the first signal. The Ops. room had picked up radio traffic over Sicily which suggested that a raid was in the offing.

The sun beat down on the pilots. It was like being in an oven. The fitters had spread damp canvas over the hoods to give them some sort of protection, before themselves taking shelter in the shade under the wings. Everything seemed to dance in the heat waves rising from the baked earth. Several hundred soldiers and Maltese, sweat pouring off them, were at work trying to repair the damage of the morning's raid. In spite of their primitive tools, the runway was quickly patched up.

What heat! And at 20,000 feet there were going to be 27 degrees of frost, but a stroke would be the result if they put on fur-lined boots or anything in the shape of underclothes now.

Feeling slightly dizzy, Beurling tried to recall the advice given to him by Grant, his Squadron-Leader, and Beverley Hill, his Section-Leader. Necessary advice too, as here you were always outnumbered ten to one!

Anyhow, this was it! This was what he had begged those hours of flying for, in Canada, when he was a kid. Those hours of flying he had paid for by leaving school and selling papers ten hours a day in the snow, half-starving—ten dollars per sixty intoxicating minutes in an old 120-h.p. Rambler. It was for this moment in

Malta that he had worked as a stoker in a broken-down Chilean cargo ship, to pay for his passage to England. For this he had put up with everything, the long hours with textbooks at Buxton-on-Sea while the other chaps went out with the girls, the scarcely veiled jeers of the maths and navigation instructors at his ignorance. For Sergeant Beurling, this was the pay-off.

He was brought back to the present by his fitter shouting: 'Scramble! Gozo at 20,000 feet!'

The perspex hood closed over him—at Luqa you had to start up your engines and take off with the hood shut because of the dust. The green rocket from the control truck was still in the air as the last Spit's engine started up.

As they climbed, the Spitfires, in three widely spaced sections of four—the famous Malta formation—described a wide spiral, crossing and recrossing every 360 degrees. Beurling was Beverley Hill's No. 2, and by careful flying he kept just fifty yards from his leader.

The pilots began to look for the enemy. A methodical search—a look to the left, to the right, above, a quick lift of the nose of the plane to see behind, a waggle of the wings to see down properly.

24,000 feet. Malta was now nothing but a featureless pancake on the sea, small enough to be hidden by one wing. A smell of hot oil, rubber and nervous sweat.

'Salmon Leader, Timber calling. 20 plus big boys at 18,000, and 40 plus fighters 15 miles out above. Gain angels quickly.'

Sixty to twelve—not too long odds, for Malta. Usually four Spits had to take on about fifty Jerries. Would there be time to get above the fighters of the escort? That was the crucial point, otherwise it would be a 'dicey' do. Unfortunately, not a wisp of cirrus to take refuge in anywhere in the whole clear expanse of blue sky.

'Aircraft 11 o'clock, slightly below Salmon!'

He pressed on the rudder-bar to shift the bulging nose of his plane and have a look in front and, sure enough, there were four viper-like shapes slipping between sky and earth towards the Salmon planes.

Where were the enemy fighters? There!—still far off, up above, a mass of elongated metallic dots, in a loose scythe-shaped formation. There was no possibility now of attacking out of the sun, according to the book. It was chiefly a question of doing something damn quick.

'Salmon Red going down. Blue and Yellow, top cover.'

The vipers had each broken up into the outlines of five separate Junkers, serenely sailing past, 3000 feet below. The four Spits of Red section dived after them.

Beverley Hill, followed by Beurling and the other six Spitfires in line astern, carried out a steep 360-degree turn and the formation fanned out to block the Messerschmitts' path as they came skimming down like a shoal of fish.

Now for it, he thought, as the enemy approached, with their long yellow fuselages spotted green and ochre and ringed with black crosses, their square cockpits, their slender wings set far forward. Con trails streamed from the wing-tips of the foremost as they straightened out and did a stall turn.

It was every man for himself now.

His hand gripping the throttle, his feet braced against the rudder-bar, his head craned forward, 'Screwball' came at the Messerschmitts at a tangent, cutting the line in half. The rear planes broke upwards. Jammed against his seat by. the centrifugal force, he turned towards a 109 who was waggling his wings undecidedly. He felt the shudder of his cannon—missed him, too much correction. A steep climb, a half-roll, stick back, and he was diving on his back with gritted teeth towards another 109 who was broadside on, turning on his ailerons.

This time he got him in his sights, steadying his plane carefully, but at the precise moment he was about to shoot the Messerschmitt skidded to one side and, like a boxer avoiding a novice's straight left, the German slipped away. A fleeting glimpse of black crosses, then nothing.

Beurling took a deep whiff of oxygen and did a roll off the top to regain height. Just as the Spitfire was hanging on its propeller, a series of flashes appeared in a corner of his mirror, crossed it, crossed back. He skidded frantically out of the way. His opponent was taken by surprise in his rum and overshot him, passing him ten yards away.

It was a Macchi 202, graceful and well proportioned, with its rounded back and tiny wings, the black *fasces* showing up sharply on the red-and-white roundels. The pilot had throttled back as far as he could—his exhausts were belching blue flame—and he was trying to get over on his back to remedy his mistake. With a violent kick Beurling swung the nose of his plane straight at the Macchi spread-eagled almost motionless in the air.

The recoil made the Spitfire stall, but the Macchi was hit. The shells—probably from only one cannon, as he was too close for them all to bear—had ripped the fuselage just behind the pilot and there was an explosion at the wing root. The Macchi remained suspended for one moment, the Spitfire falling past him dangerously close. Then one wing dropped and the Italian went into a spin, surrounded with white glycol vapour.

A cluster of three parachutes floated in the middle of a swarm of aircraft—the crew of a Junkers 88. Above Beurling whirled a chain of planes—Spits and Messerschmitts alternately—twisting and twining round a formation of five Junkers 88s, patiently waiting their chance to dive.

Five grey Messerschmitts in close line-astern formation were diving in a curve as graceful as a scimitar on the Hurricanes from Takali, who were climbing flat out to join the scrap.

Beurling tried to warn them, but in vain. They were probably on a different channel. He tried to intercept the enemy, but it was too late. There was a brief flash of Mausers, the sword-thrust of tracer, and a Hurricane gently turned over on its back, the pilot blindly trying to regain control. Then down he went, leaving a thin trail of black smoke behind him.

The Messerschmitt responsible was immediately attacked by a Spitfire, its guns blazing. Beurling swung away from them and veered to the right to get back over Malta. Still with full boost, he plunged at 500 m.p.h. after a line of Junkers 88s diving with their big bombs under the wings. Their dive-brakes were down and he caught up fast.

A glance at the mirror this time—all clear. Describing a perfect curve, he closed with the rearmost Junkers 88. The tracer from its dorsal turret flitted like sparks over the Spit. It was Screwball's first shot at a bomber.

His sight framed the bulging cockpit, the slender fuselage with its tail fin, the Jumo engines with their long circular cowlings and the trapezoidal wings. A bit more correction . . . range eighty yards . . . the smack of an enemy bullet . . . nothing to worry about, only a 7.7 . . . 10 degrees, one rad deflection. This time Beurling did not miss. There was a flood of smoke, followed by long straight spurts of flame licking at the tailplane. Perspex panels fluttered down. A dark shape emerged, then another—the crew jumping.

'Help! Can't land. One-o-nines patrolling Hal Far.'

It was Billy the Kid's voice. He was probably running out of juice, and trying to land with 109s about would be asking for it. Beurling let go the Junkers 88, which was finished anyway, turned over on his back and dived vertically for the sea. Skimming the waves, and hugging the cliffs to keep out of sight, he flew to the rescue. He was getting short of juice too, anyway.

There was the beached wreck of the transport, Hal Far must be just behind. Suddenly puffs of A.A. appeared from nowhere and hung over the cliff. Three Messerschmitts roared over from the plateau, without seeing him, as he was in the shadows a few feet from the beach. They turned away from him, preparing for another run over the airfield. Beurling leapt to the attack, turned inside them and fired on the foremost. It was a difficult target—nearly 60 degrees correction—but the short burst hammered home and the Messerschmitt tilted over and crashed into the ruins of a chapel.

'Try to keep Safi strip clear while I glide in.'

'O.K.'

For the next thirty seconds it was up to him. Once Billy was on the ground the Bofors would do the rest.

Over Safi there was an absolute rodeo going on. Messerschmitts were haring about all over the place, preventing a desperate Spitfire with its undercart down from landing. It was probably Billy, and he was having to keep on turning, too tightly for the Jerries to catch him.

'All right, Billy. Nip in, here I come!'

Billy caught on all right and throttled back without a moment's hesitation. If the manoeuvre was not perfectly synchronised he was a dead duck—the Messerschmitts would not miss him. He side-slipped steeply, straightened out at the last moment, and put her down. Beurling came rocketing across the perimeter and attacked head-on a Messerschmitt 109 already over the runway and preparing to machine-gun Billy's plane on the ground.

The Messerschmitt, taken by surprise, broke sharply and the two planes crossed a few feet apart at 600 m.p.h. Crash! Beurling felt a thud at the back of his neck and his cockpit filled with smoke. On the cowling, between himself and the engine, there were two long gashes made by armour-piercing shells. But the Messerschmitt, unable to follow the Spit as it turned, skimming the bomb-craters with its wing-tip, broke off.

Four Spitfires called back by Control now appeared to clean up the circuit. The Messerschmitt 109s dived over the cliff and shot off over the sea in the direction of Sicily.

Pushing hard with both hands, Beurling slid back his hood. Undercart down, engine throttled back, propeller at fine pitch, flaps down, he made his approach. He must keep his eyes open for the craters so liberally scattered over the runway by the Junkers 88s.

The Spitfire was now bumping safely on the ground, on its narrow undercart. He braked to avoid the still smoking debris of a Spitfire. At last, the rabbit burrow, and the fitter signalling him in.

Phew! What a party! He was soaked with sweat, which ran into his eyes, down his neck, under his armpits, everywhere.

His first show over Malta: two for certain—one Messerschmitt 109 and one Junkers 88—and one probable, the Macchi 202.

An hour later, his plane refuelled and rearmed, Beurling took off again with another flight to intercept a formation of thirty Junkers 87 Stukas, escorted by one hundred and ten Messerschmitts! The Luftwaffe at all costs meant to sink the *Welshman*, which had just arrived with a cargo of aviation spirit and A.A. ammunition. Every Spitfire and Hurricane on the island that was capable of flying at all went up.

A terrific scrap developed over Valetta, joined rather clumsily by about thirty Macchi 202s. The Stukas, superbly flown, dived hell for leather through the A.A. barrage, pursued by the Spits, who were themselves deluged by an avalanche of enemy fighters.

Beurling brought down one Messerschmitt 109 and fired at point-blank range on a Junkers 87 which had just dropped its 1000-lb. bomb. He was so close to his opponent that the Stuka's hood, ripped off by his shells, smashed his propeller. An A.S.R.

launch which was just below the fight followed him at full speed, but Beurling miraculously righted his plane and belly-landed it on a tiny field near a lighthouse.

That evening, in spite of the smell of petrol and the discomfort of the Mess, Beurling ate heartily and slept sound. He had shown his incomparable virtuosity on the very first day. The sacrifices of his youth had not been in vain.

CHAPTER FOUR

ADMIRAL YAMAMOTO

May 1940, Bering Sea

Overtaken by a tornado near Matthew Island, a Japanese seal-hunting ship had sunk. Three days later a Norwegian whaler picked up the Japanese skipper's body, floating on the surface in a lifebelt.

The identity and other papers found on the body were carefully put aside, for handing to the authorities at Nackneck at the end of the whaling season. The Norwegians had also found a book—at first sight a series of mathematical or logarithm tables—which had a curious binding of cloth-covered lead. The body was sewn in a weighted sack and lowered into the sea, while the skipper read the prayer for the dead.

A week later they sighted an American fishery protection vessel, hailed it, and handed over the papers, a report and the book. The American skipper, an officer in the U.S. Naval Reserve, leapt a yard in the air when he saw the book of tables and immediately made full steam for Dutch Harbour, where a big naval base was being constructed.

The little book was nothing less than the Japanese Imperial Navy's basic code.

The possession of such a precious book by a mere seal-hunter was incidentally not particularly surprising. The crews of Japanese—and Russian—trawlers and so on were stiff with regular naval officers taking photos and soundings in Alaskan waters.

As Frank Knox, Secretary of the Navy, later wrote: 'This discovery meant for us the equivalent of an extra battle fleet.'

Working from this basic code, which was common to the Air Force, the Navy, and the Foreign Ministry (oddly enough the Army had a totally different code which defied all the efforts of the experts to crack it), the Americans were to all intents and purposes able to follow the Japs' every move. A special branch to deal just with this code was set up in the White House until the declaration of war. Only President Roosevelt and Cordell Hull had access to it. The President therefore knew, before even the Japanese ambassador in Washington, all Tokyo's instructions to its diplomatic services during those tragic weeks in October and November and up to 7th December 1941. He even had advance information of the attack on Pearl Harbor as far back as the 28th of November. But that is another story.

It was thanks to this code that the most extraordinary man-hunt in the entire Pacific war was organised. The object of this hunt was Admiral Isoroku Yamamoto, Commander-in-Chief of the Imperial Japanese Navy.

Yamamoto, a naval tactician of genius whom history will rank with Togo and Nelson, was the moving spirit and driving force in the Japanese armed forces. He was quite young—not yet fifty—knew the United States intimately, and had always been opposed to the desire for war as expressed by the Tojo-Matsuoka faction. He was an influential friend of Prince Konoye's and had written to him at the beginning of 1940: 'If in spite of everything I have to fight, then all must be over in six months or a year: I cannot take responsibility for a two-year war against the United States. I am against the Tripartite Pact and always have been. But now it is too late. I hope our government will avoid a war against the United States.'

Seeing that war was inevitable, he drew up the masterly plan of campaign which in the event enabled the Japanese to win the battle of the Pacific in twelve months. It was from his flagship, the battleship *Yamato*, that was flashed the signal *Niitaka Yama Nobore*, which let loose the attack on Pearl Harbor.

It was particularly during the Guadalcanal campaign that the full extent of his genius was revealed to the Americans.

Guadalcanal is a small island lost in the Solomons Archipelago, 1200 miles north of Australia. Ten square miles of fetid jungle and stinking malaria-infested mud, fringed by a thin line of coconut-palms along the marshy beaches. A tropical hell, shunned by men ever since 7th February 1568, when Don Alvaro Mendana planted there the standard of His Most Catholic Majesty.

On 4th July 1942 a Flying Fortress, coming back from a recce trip over Tulagi, was blown off course by a storm and flew over Guadalcanal at 23,000 feet. The observer took a few photos on the off-chance. When the plates were developed all hell was let loose in Admiral Nimitz's G.H.Q. There was no getting away from the photographic evidence. The Japs had landed troops on Guadalcanal on the quiet and had started building an airfield.

85

This modest field, a mere landing-strip hacked out of the jungle, was destined to upset all the Americans' plans.

On 7th August 1942, 11,000 Marines made a surprise landing on Lunga Point, and as early as the following evening they had captured the landing-strip, which they named Henderson Field. In theory the capture of the island was only a question of days and no one could guess that a tiny third-class military operation like that would develop into a bitter series of land, air and naval engagements.

Yamamoto calmly followed the American move from Truk, where he had immediately gone, on board the *Yamato*. He let the Americans get really committed, then moved to the attack. For him it was a heaven-sent locale for a war of attrition against the U.S., in that maze of islands where the superiority of his crews and of his strategy would have a real chance to show themselves.

When on 7th February 1943 at 4.15 p.m. the last Jap soldier on Guadalcanal was finally dead, the American Navy had fought six major naval battles in the waters round that accursed island. Of the six, four were defeats and two were inconclusive. In these battles—Savo on 9th August 1942, Eastern Solomons on 24th August, Cape of Hope on the night of llth-12th September, Santa Cruz Islands on 26th and 28th October, Guadalcanal on the night of 12th-13th November, and Tassafaronga on 30th November—the American Navy lost two of its precious aircraft-carriers, the *Wasp* and the *Hornet*, six heavy cruisers, two light cruisers and fourteen destroyers, not to mention a certain number of heavy units temporarily put out of action.

In all these battles, in spite of superiority in numbers, gunpower, radar and aircraft, thanks to which losses were kept within bounds, the American Navy was tactically outclassed by the Japanese, who scrupulously followed Yamamoto's instructions.

For instance, at Tassafaronga, Task Force 67, warned in advance by its reconnaissance planes, set a trap with five heavy cruisers and six destroyers for a Japanese force which consisted of a mere seven destroyers. The Japanese destroyers laboured under the further handicap of carrying ammunition and 5000 drums of petrol for their beleaguered garrison on Guadalcanal, and also large numbers of troops who crowded the decks and blocked the alley-ways. After a vicious engagement in the dark lasting thirty minutes, one of the American cruisers, the *Northampton,* was sunk, and the four others, *New Orleans*, *Pensacola*, *Portland* and *Minneapolis*, were out of action. The last two were practically cut in half and only saved by a miracle. The Japanese, following Yamamoto's pre-arranged plan, j suffered no losses during the engagement itself.

Yamamoto became the Americans' *bête noire* in the Pacific, as did Rommel for the British in Libya.

* * *

The U.S. Navy's reception post at Dutch Harbour was deep in underground concrete shelters. Up above on the cliffs rose the seven enormous 300-foot radio masts. The Japs frequently tried to destroy them.

On 17th April 1943 at 6.36 a.m. a coded signal from Truk was intercepted. As it had the call-sign of the *Yamato*, Admiral Yamamoto's flagship, it was relayed to Washington with top priority, via Kiska, Kodiak, Elmendorf and San Francisco. At Arlington Hall the cryptographers immediately got busy over the groups . . . 28743253 54178932 72918376 . . . (Next door the finishing touches were being put to the first electronic brain, which within a few months took over all the donkey work. The basic elements of the Japanese code were fed in at one end, the intercepted message at the other, and in a matter of minutes the machine produced the answer in clear.)

At 11 o'clock the translated message was on Frank Knox's desk, just as he returned from a sitting of the Senate. The Secretary of State read the message, a current one giving an itinerary for a tour of inspection by Yamamoto. As it was just a routine message, devoid of any tactical or strategic interest, Knox went off to lunch. During the meal a casual remark by his private Secretary—the old theory that wars could be settled by individual duels between commanders; no commanders no wars—was the starting-point for the extraordinary affair which bore the cover-name of Operation Vengeance.

Might it not be possible to intercept Yamamoto with fighter aircraft and shoot him down? It might change the whole course of the war in the Pacific!

Knox immediately alerted General Arnold, Commander-in-Chief of the Army Air Force, who in turn sent for Colonel Charles Lindbergh, a specialist on long-distance flights with P-38s, and Frank Meyer, from Lockheed's experimental department.

A rapid study of maps and distances showed that it might well be possible, using P-38s from Guadalcanal, to intercept the Admiral over Kahili airfield the next morning at 9.45. But only if special auxiliary tanks could be got out to them in time.

At 3.35 p.m. two signals went out, signed personally by Frank Knox. One was for General Kenney, in command of the Air Forces in the S.W. Pacific, in Australia. This one concerned the auxiliary tanks. The other was relayed by Pearl Harbor direct to the Fighter Control Centre, Henderson Field, on Guadalcanal.

The Kenney signal was passed on to the 13th U.S. Air Force Ordnance Depot at Port Moresby. Three hours later four four-engined Liberators took off from Milne Bay with eighteen 310-gallon drop-tanks and eighteen 165-gallon ones, for Henderson Field.

The signal for Henderson Field reached Guadalcanal at 4 p.m., but just then there was a raid by Japanese planes. Marine pilots took off in Corsairs to beat them off and in the ensuing battle one Corsair crashed close to the airfield and its pilot was burnt to cinders before the eyes of the appalled personnel of the airfield. In the event Major Mitchell, commanding 339 Squadron (P-38s), was only called at 5.10 p.m.

A jeep from Fighter Control collected him and his two Flight-Leaders, Lieutenants Thomas G. Lanphier and Beasby Holmes. All along the nine-mile stretch of road from Henderson to Tassafaronga there were ample signs of the fierce battles that had followed the landings.

The Navy and Army H.Q. at Tassafaronga was hidden in a palm-grove, the buildings half buried in the sand. Water had oozed in and formed puddles on the floors. Twenty or so officers were squelching about, talking eagerly. The signal received read: 'Washington, 17.4.43, 15.35. Top Secret, Secretary Navy to Fighter Control Henderson.

'Admiral Yamamoto accompanied chief of staff and seven general officers imperial navy including surgeon admiral grand fleet left Truk this morning eight hours for air trip inspection Bougainville bases stop Admiral and party travelling in two Sallys escorted six Zekes stop escort of honour from Kahili probable stop admiral's itinerary colon arrive Rabaul Bucka I 1630 hours where spend night stop leave dawn for Kahili where time of arrival 0945 hours stop admiral then to board submarine chaser for inspection naval units under admiral Tanaka stop.

'Squadron 339 P-38 must at all costs reach and destroy Yamamoto and staff morning april eighteen stop auxiliary tanks and consumption data will arrive from Port Moresby evening seventeenth stop intelligence stresses admirals extreme punctuality stop president attaches extreme importance this operation stop communicate result at once Washington stop Frank Knox Secretary of State for Navy.

'Ultra-secret document, not to be copied or filed. To be destroyed when carried out.'

Mitchell, the flimsy still in his hand, whistled through his teeth after a look at the map covering the big table.

550 miles! 1100 miles there and back, with a probable scrap into the bargain. At least five hours' flying, as they would have to fly at economical cruising speed. Sounded like a shaky do. To add to his doubts, the signal from Port Moresby confirming

despatch of the auxiliary tanks made it clear that only eighteen planes could be fitted out. What would happen if that escort of honour consisted of forty Zeros?

The discussion over the final plan of action lasted until dinner, a frugal one on Guadalcanal—canned sausages and biscuits, plus a glass of canned orange juice for the pilots only. The Navy officers suggested waiting until Yamamoto was on board his submarine chaser, and then sinking it. Holmes retorted that a normal fighter-pilot wouldn't pretend to be able to identify that one boat from among the hundreds dotted about the bay. Anyway, even if you machine-gunned the survivors in the sea one by one, you still would not be certain that Yamamoto had been liquidated. Besides—conclusive argument—there would be naval A.A. No thanks!

Then again, how could they make certain of intercepting him in the air? Provided Yamamoto was punctual they would have to jump him thirty miles or so east of Kahili. Counting about four miles to the minute, contact would have to be made at roughly 9.35.

At what height would he be flying? An important point as, although the met. people promised clear weather, atmospheric conditions in the tropics were pretty unstable. It seemed likely that the two bombers would fly fairly low, say 10,000 feet, to relieve the V.I.P.s on board of the discomfort of wearing oxygen masks.

Finally it was all settled, and Mitchell agreed, rather unwillingly, to lead the twelve P-38s which would fly at 20,000 feet to provide top-cover for the other six. These, the ones who would have the tricky job of making the actual interception, would fly at 11,000 feet. Take-off was fixed for 7.20 a.m.

The choice of pilots was going to be difficult. The squadron had forty, and those not chosen were obviously going to scream blue murder. In the end they decided to draw lots among the twenty-five most experienced.

At 9 p.m., just before a terrific thunderstorm broke, the four Liberators bringing the auxiliary tanks made a rather rocky landing on the small and inadequately lit strip at Henderson Field. The fitters set to work in the torrential rain and pitch darkness by the light of electric torches—the Jap bombers constantly circling the island were in the habit of dropping their bombs on any light suggesting activity; It was a hellish job fitting those drop-tanks between the two engine-booms and the cockpit. They were too big and heavy, for one thing, and everything had to be improvised. They worked feverishly, up to the ankles in mud, and surrounded by swarms of malaria mosquitoes attracted by the light of the torches.

16th April 1943

The radiant sun rose in a limpid sky. All the pilots of 339 had been at Dispersal since 6 o'clock. Those who were going hid whatever apprehension they might feel under a jaunty manner, fiddling about with their planes and making last-minute suggestions to the fitters. The moment before taking off for a trip is always poignant. You adjust your parachute as you stand on the wing, and take what may be your last look at all the familiar things—-your friends, the flight-hut with its walls plastered with pin-ups, its maps and blackboards, and the table where you have so often played poker and staked the money you hadn't got. The fitter hides what he feels by giving the perspex of your hood an extra polish.

Major Mitchell arrived at last, his face drawn and unshaven— he had spent the night supervising the fitters' work. He called the pilots round him, and, sitting on the bonnet of the jeep leaning on his parachute, gave them their final instructions.

'Doug Cannings and I, each with a section of six planes, will try to protect the intercepting force from the Zeros of the escort. Thomas Lanphier, Rex Barber, Beasby Holmes, Ray Hine, Joe Moore and James MacLanahan will therefore be free for the job of going after the bombers, who have got to be brought down at all costs. Whatever happens, dive through the Zeros, take no notice of them.'

7.20 a.m.—One engine fired, coughing oil-laden smoke, through the exhausts, then another . . . three . . . seven . . . ten— thirty-six Allisons roaring. The Major's P-38 started rolling on the steel tracking of the strip, as graceful on its three slender legs as a ballerina on her toes. One by one the heavily laden P-38s took off, with the usual shrill whine of superchargers.

MacLanahan's plane burst a tyre at 100 m.p.h., skidded on the damp tracking, smashed its undercart and crashed at the end of the runway in a sea of flames. The pilot jumped unhurt out of the cockpit and removed himself at record speed before the final explosion.

Joe Moore switched over to his auxiliary tank, but he felt a sudden loss of power and at the same time the boost gauge showed a violent drop. No juice coming through. He quickly switched back to his wing tanks, then tried the drop-tank again, although he was low over the water. Risky, but he didn't want to miss the trip. It was no good, the engines died on him again and, pumping like a madman, he only just succeeded in starting up again in time on the wing-tanks. He had to turn back.

The remaining sixteen P-38s in three sections, one of four planes and two of six, lost Guadalcanal behind them in the dry morning mist.

It was a picture-postcard morning—little emerald-green islands fringed with mother-of-pearl in a sea as calm as the proverbial mill-pond.

For the pilots, in spite of the danger, every trip was a holiday, as it was an escape from Guadalcanal. Now that you were away from the fetid marshes and the stench of the jungle, those islands etched in the warm, shimmering air represented an in-accessible earthly paradise with their golden sands, scarlet creepers and indigo trees.

Giving the Japanese-held archipelagos a wide berth, the pilots left on the right first Munda, then Rendova, Vella Lavelle and Shortland. They were flying too low and too far out to be picked up by Japanese radar.

The sun was beginning to beat through the perspex. Tommy Lanphier, in shirt-sleeves, was sweating. He could feel the drops forming under his armpits and trickling coldly down his sides.

Nearly two hours of flying already and strict R/T. silence all the time. The whine of the superchargers on either side of the cockpit was beginning to stupefy him. The pilots, hunched up for too long, were screwing about in their cockpits to avoid cramp.

'We're going to miss them,' thought Lanphier. 'It would be too good to be true if we didn't. Things like that only happen on the movies.' Below to the right, sliding under the tailplane, was the tip of Bougainville. Soon be time to start climbing.

9.30 a.m.—The 310-gallon tank was a terrible nuisance. As it had no internal partitions the petrol inside sloshed about, and the pilot had the disagreeable impression every five seconds of getting a kick in the nose of his plane. Any attempt to check the movement only made matters worse.

9.33 a.m.—There they go! Mitchell's boys started climbing, their shadows still following them on the waves. The P-38s went up at an incredible angle, their noses pointing straight up at the sun and apparently hung on invisible threads. In one movement Lanphier opened up to 2600 revs—mixture fully rich, thirty-four inches of boost. The four Lightnings of the attack section rose. Every eye scanned the sky. Tommy swept the sky carefully up to the level of the sun, his hand shielding his eyes.

'Not a thing. How the boys will . . .'

'Look out! Bogys ten o'clock high!'

It was Canning's voice, quite calm, but Tommy jumped as if he had had an electric shock. There they were, coming towards them, above and a bit to the left. The admiral was on time.

3000 revs, combat pitch, combat flaps—so many things to do with your hands, while you kept the stick wedged with your knees—petrol cocks over to wing-tanks, now then, what about the drop-tanks; mustn't forget how you get rid of the 310-gallon one—keep that ball in the middle, no skidding . . . the plane, relieved of its load, leapt forward. It all had to be done by feel while you kept your eyes fixed on the bright dots, now immediately above.

Holmes had mucked it up and the 310-gallon tank had hit his tailplane as it fell, and on top of that he couldn't shake off the 165-gallon one.

A turn, then they climbed, practically parallel with the enemy, who seemed to have noticed nothing yet. They must stay out of sight in the blind spot formed by the wings.

Barber was still with Lanphier, but the Holmes-Hinc section had vanished.

The two Lightnings were now only 1000 feet below the two Sallys. One of the planes was a uniform khaki colour, the other was bright grey with irregular olive-green camouflage stripes. The big red dies of the rising sun showed up clearly. This second Sally was closely escorted by six Zeros, three on each side. It must be Yamamoto's.

A left turn to get between the enemy formation and the island, and suddenly the Zeros dropped their tanks, which went fluttering down. The three first Zeros attacked the two Lightnings head on, at a relative speed of 750 m.p.h. Long bursts of tracer crossed, and a green and yellow Zero, shaken by the stream of steel poured out by the 13-mm. machine-guns and the 20-mm. cannon, turned on its back and shot past Lanphier's aircraft.

The two Sallys now knew the score and were diving towards the island. Tommy went after them. But the Zeros were extraordinarily quick off the mark, probably crack pilots. The three others in perfect close formation did an impeccable loop and veered to cut him off while the two first did such a tight turn that he gained little ground on them. The Zeros and the Lightning converged on the camouflaged Sally. It was a race to the death, with the bomber as prize. The brain works fast at such moments, but an experienced pilot's reflexes work faster than thought. Like a wing forward on a football field Lanphier feinted and caught the Zeros on the wrong foot—he pretended to turn left, putting an exaggerated bank, and immediately the two Zeros swung towards him and, as they neared, the first opened fire . . . a brutal kick on the left rudder bar to slip under the tracer, and then stick hard right and over he went in a barrel roll. He shot under the two Zeros and dived towards the bombers like a bat out of hell.

Barber had kept straight on and had opened fire on the three other Zeros, who broke and faced him. Tommy went slap through them at full throttle and found himself in the slipstream of the nearer of the Sallys. It was the camouflaged one, Yamamoto's. At 400 m.p.h. hunter and hunted roared down towards the jungle-covered island. The Sally loomed up in the sights, the two engines clearly visible with their white-hot exhausts. The gun turrets were not even manned.

Tommy trembled with excitement as he pressed the button. The recoil of the 20-mm. cannon and the four 13-mm. machine-guns between his legs made the stick shake in his gloved hand. A smell of powder invaded the cockpit.

The Sally straightened out and the Lightning went on firing, weaving from left to right to avoid the dangerous wake from the propellers . . . a long burst. . . the shells exploded in the treetops and got closer to the shadow of the plane jumping from tree to tree. A hit, on the starboard engine! First a thin dark trail then a ring of flame round the cowling. Plates flew off the wing, releasing an enormous plume of black smoke. The Sally, one wing in flames, lost speed and Tommy lowered his flaps ten more degrees and throttled right back.

A second burst to finish him off. Nobody would be able to jump, the plane was too low. The Sally brushed the tops of the trees, skidded suddenly, a wing caught and folded up in a shower of purple flames, sparks and debris. The blazing fuselage carved its way through the trees. Not much doubt about that!

A glance at the mirror—here come the Zeros! A vertical climb, which the Japanese fighters with their controls stiffened by the speed could not hope to follow without their wings folding up. The Lightning, climbing full boost, flew over Kahili airfield. Zeros were taking off in all directions in a cloud of dust.

A few haphazard bursts from 75-mm. A.A. and that was all. In the meantime Barber had been rescued by Mitchell and the covering sections from a dozen Zeros which had suddenly appeared from nowhere. He managed to overhaul the second bomber, which was making for the beach at sea-level. The bursts from the Lightning tore a strip of foam from the sea which gradually caught up with the Sally. The Jap plane crashed into a coral reef with a terrific explosion. One Lightning, an engine on fire, went down in a spin and crashed near a jutting crag. It was Hine, who had sacrificed himself to protect Holmes by taking on three Zeros in a dog-fight.

In spite of the handicap of his drop-tank and his damaged tailplane, Holmes had got one Zero for certain plus one probable. Barber was trying to finish this one off when Mitchell suddenly gave the order for immediate return. Six Lightnings were badly damaged and two had to toil painfully back on one engine, the other propeller feathered. Mission completed. The manhunt was over.

Yamamoto's charred body was found in the debris of the Sally. The Admiral died leaning on the hilt of his Samurai sword, which was brought back to Tokio for an impressive military funeral.

Lieutenant Lanphier was promoted to the rank of Captain and received the Navy Cross and a personal telegram of congratulations from President Roosevelt. His exploit was not officially announced until 1st September 1945, as his brother Charles, who had been shot down at Bataan, was a prisoner in Japanese hands and the American government feared possible reprisals.

History may say one day that Yamamoto's death was Japan's first great defeat in the 1941-45 war.

NOTE ON THE LOCKHEED P-38 'LIGHTNING'

The Two-Tailed Devil—Der Gabelschwanzteufel, as the Germans called it—was one of the best known aircraft of the last war. Its distinctive outline and the characteristic whine of its superchargers will remain indelibly associated in French memory with the stirring weeks of May and June 1944.

The Lightning can certainly claim to have been the most discussed aircraft among Allied fighter-pilots. It was loathed by some, but by others it was put on a level with the Spitfire, which was rather an exaggerated compliment.

The story of this remarkable plane begins in 1937. The U.S. Army Air Corps had issued a schedule of requirements for a fast twin-engined single seater fighter with a large radius of action. It was at that time that vague mentions of the Messerschmitt 110 were beginning to seep through via the ultra-secret reports of air attaches with the Berlin embassies. France had already shown very pretty twin-engined fighters, the Henriot and the Potez 63 at the 1936 Air Show. Fokker in Holland was building his G.I.

In a word, the fashion—Just as exacting in aircraft design as in ladies' hats—was for this kind of plane.

The requirements were very stiff—360 m.p.h. at 20,000 feet and a radius of action of 300 miles—and they were enough to put off the majority of American designers. Among the firms that tendered designs was Lockheeds, a small, young firm. It had a mere thousand or so workmen and technicians and had up till then produced only five types of aircraft amounting to a total of 107 light transport planes, including the successful Lockheed 12 'Electra'.

Business was not too good—France and Britain had not yet begun to place orders in America—and this possible contract became a question of life and death for the firm. All production ceased and the drawing-office set to work. Every possible layout, even the most revolutionary, was considered in turn—two engines in tandem, engines with indirect transmission, etc., etc.

The chief problem was where to put the two cumbersome G.E.C. exhaust impellers. If they were put in the fuselage the result was a monstrosity, quite apart from the probability of the pilot being roasted alive. If they went behind the engines, the shaft would mess up the trailing edge of the wing. Finally the only logical conclusion was reached by sheer elimination; suppress the main fuselage and extend the engine units by means of two booms which would carry the tailplane.

The cockpit 'egg', containing the pilot and the armament specified—four machine-guns and one 23-mm. Madsen cannon—was placed in the nose. The wing, incidentally, was a very successful design, and an enlarged version was eventually used in that superb plane, the Constellation. Finally, as a last bold stroke, a tricycle undercarriage was designed, the first to be fitted to any American plane.

When the blue-prints and the scale model were finished, the Air Corps technicians came to examine them. After shying at first—officials on principle dislike accepting revolutionary ideas— they placed an order for a prototype. This was in June 1937.

The young Lockheed engineers now had to face a series of resounding technical setbacks. The first wing behaved disquietingly in the wind-tunnel. A second, designed and constructed in eighteen days, could not take normal flaps at more than 110 m.p.h. without an alarming change of attitude. Finally Fowler came to the rescue with his variable aspect-ratio flaps, which had just saved another of the firm's initial failures, the Lockheed 14, from which the R.A.F. Hudson was later derived.

The front wheel of the tricycle undercart, when it was tested under a two-ton weight towed at 75 m.p.h., developed a terrifying judder, and, to cap all, the two prototype engines—900-h.p. Allisons—proved to be extremely temperamental on the test bench.

As the Lockheed team were really keen, they did not let all this get them down. The firm even managed to dig out a test-pilot from among the out-of-work suicide specialists from the Cleveland Air Races.

At last, on 27th January 1939, Lieutenant on Reserve (now Colonel) Ben F. Kesley, succeeded in getting the XP-38 into the air, watched by the chief engineer, Hall Hibbart, and the entire personnel massed at the foot of the control tower on March Field in California.

Just as they were all patting each other on the back over a perfect take-off, the trouble began. As Kesley tried to pick up his flaps, a control-rod came unstuck. Shaken by terrific vibrations, the plane started to swing all over the place. The pilot hesitated whether to bale out, but obeying the unwritten code, 'bring the kite home at all costs,' decided to try to land her. By an incredible feat of airmanship he succeeded in putting her down all of a piece in a ploughed field on a hillside.

The plane was repaired and the next ten flights went off without a hitch. In the meantime, however, the Air Corps technicians had changed their minds and announced that they did not now intend to persevere with the project. Lockheeds decided that drastic measures were called for, and on 11th February Ben Kesley took off from March Field for New York. Beating all transcontinental records, Kesley was over Long Island in seven hours and two minutes. Tired by his journey, and the exceptionally difficult atmospheric conditions, Kesley throttled back too far when he came in to land and flooded his engines when he opened up again too roughly. Left with two dead engines, he had to belly-land in a ravine.

The only witness of the accident telephoned the press first and the airfield second, in the best American tradition. The next day's papers were plastered with photographs of the XP-38, and the first result of this unforeseen publicity was, curiously enough, an initial order for thirteen aircraft.

The technical big-shots whose hand had been thus forced got their own back by inflicting on Lockheed's poor harassed engineers no fewer than 3897 modifications. It was therefore not till July 1941 that the first P-38 came off the assembly line.

The first forty were sent to the R.A.F. under Lease-Lend, but minus their superchargers, as these were still considered to be top-secret. As without them the P-38 was practically useless, the R.A.F. politely but firmly declined to use its pilots as guinea-pigs on them (just as it did with the P-39 Airacobra). The P-38 therefore continued to be produced for the exclusive use of the U.S. Army Air Corps.

Then the war caught up with the United States, and the first operational flight on a P-38 was carried out in June 1942 by a Captain Karl Polifka. It was a reconnaissance flight over the Japanese fleet, from Australia. After that the P-38 totally vanished from circulation and was not heard of again till the North African landing in November 1942, when the name 'Lightning' began to figure in communiqués.

Its beginnings were not too brilliant. The American pilots not only lacked combat experience, they had not quite got the hang of their twin-engined machines, and furthermore suffered from a pronounced feeling of inferiority *vis-à-vis* single-engine fighters. The Focke-Wulfs had a wonderful time. The first three P-38 squadrons were to all intents wiped out within a few weeks, and at one stage they even had to be escorted by P-40s, which could hardly keep up with them.

Gradually a special combat technique was elaborated by the Langley Field experts. Special flaps were fitted which were lowered 8 degrees during combat to facilitate turns, and fighter-pilots learned to exploit the advantage of having two engines.

Thanks to its speed, its great range and, above all, the extreme toughness and reliability of its air frame, the Lightning eventually became a firm favourite. The wings could be festooned like a Christmas tree with an assortment of auxiliary tanks, bombs, rockets, even torpedoes, according to the requirements of the moment; and of course also a collection of cameras for taking vertical and oblique photos.

Its armament being concentrated in the nose, it was ideal for strafing targets on the ground. Hence the name of 'two-tailed devil' given to it by the wretched Wehrmacht infantry, merci-lessly harried on the roads of Normandy. Its speed made it quite a respectable reconnaissance aircraft (Saint-Exupéry was flying the F.S. Photo version when he disappeared). But as a straight fighter it was never as good as the P-51, or even that big brute the P-47 Thunderbolt. A very few pilots—Bong and MacGuire in the Pacific (forty and thirty-eight successes), and Jenkins and

Thomas White in England (sixteen and twenty-two successes)—took on the standard single-engine fighters successfully, thanks to a special and difficult team-work technique, but they were exceptions. At Fassberg in 1945 I saw a combat film of Hans Phillip shooting down the four Lightnings of a section one after the other. It might have given budding P-38 pilots something to think about, but luckily the war was over.

6900 Lightnings were built, and, after successive modifications, by 1945 this aircraft—officially a fighter—could carry two tons of bombs 600 miles, i.e. half a ton more than the Flying Fortress. That represented a three-ton overload since the original blue-print.

In 1945 the P-38s engines developed 1600 h.p. each, or almost double the power of the 1938 Allisons. In March 1944 Ben Kesley dived a Lightning at 800 m.p.h. in a test. A second experiment of the same kind in May 1944 nearly ended in disaster. Kesley's wings folded up at 23,000 feet and he only managed to jump clear in the nick of time. After that he had to have six months' 'furlough' with a P-38 squadron operating in the Pacific.

The particulars of the Lockheed P-38J were as follows: wing-span 50 feet, length 38 feet, wing area 330 square feet, weight unloaded 5-7 tons, maximum loaded weight 8-2 tons; maximum speed 414 m.p.h. at 25,000 feet; radius of action without drop-tanks 360 miles; armament, four 13-mm. machine-guns and one 20-mm. Hispano cannon; all metal construction.

CHAPTER FIVE

COLONEL PIJEAUD

At the beginning of 1941 Rommel's tactical air support in Egypt consisted of sixty-five Messerschmitt 109s, eighty-four Stukas (Junkers 87s), forty-two Messerschmitt 110s (long-range fighter-bombers) and a few Junkers 88s—never more than twenty—used for armed reconnaissance. These two hundred or so aircraft were laboriously kept supplied with petrol and ammunition (German supplies of these two essentials in the desert never did reach an adequate level) by Junkers 52s and big Savoia Marchetti 82 'Kangaroos', hurriedly recalled from Crete and the Balkans.

About 250 aircraft of the Regia Aeronautica d'Italia were also available—Cant 1001s, Savoia 79s, Fiat 42s and, in addition, a handful of Macchi 202s which were, however, mostly reserved for the Battle of Malta. For special strategic operations Rommel could also call on units stationed on Rhodes.

Air-Marshal Longmore, who commanded the R.A.F. in Egypt, had an even more difficult problem than his adversary. With only a very small strength in aircraft he had to try and make up for the obvious inferiority of the British ground-forces, particularly in armour.

Longmore had under him five bomber squadrons (45,113 and

106

55 equipped with Blenheims, and 38 and 70 equipped with Wellingtons) and five fighter squadrons (3, 274, 73 and 4 'South African' equipped with Hurricanes, and 5 'South African' equipped with Tomahawks). In all sixty-eight Blenheims, twenty-nine Wellingtons, eighty-eight Hurricanes and Tomahawks and seventeen army co-operation Lysanders.

Two more bomber squadrons were added to these, both South African. One was equipped with Junkers 86s, old German planes fitted with radial engines, and the other with Glenn Martin Marylands.

With these figures in mind, one can easily appreciate the importance of the contribution made by the Free French Air Force, represented by the 'Lorraine' Squadron, equipped with Blenheims, and the GC1, a squadron of Hurricanes. In addition, Free France provided the only direct route for supplies and reinforcements. In three months no fewer than 147 aircraft were transferred to Egypt via Takoradi, while only ten Wellingtons, five Blenheims and two Beauforts had arrived via Malta.

Unfortunately, out of these 147 planes 72 were Tomahawks (Curtiss P-40s) for the Australian squadrons in process of formation, and they had to be drastically modified before they could be risked against Messerschmitt 109s. The workshops in Alexandria had to provide them with new armament, modify the cooling system, fit carburettor filters, oxygen, different sights, and improve the tail-trimmer.

During this same period the R.A.F. lost 184 planes!

These meagre R.A.F. and F.F. Air Forces had, unaided, to sustain the heroic effort on which the fate of the world struggle depended at that time. It is difficult to resist the temptation to pause and consider the attitude of the French leaders in Africa at this juncture.

In August 1940 they had at their disposal an impressive number of warplanes. In all there were fifteen fighter and bomber squadrons equipped with American planes, plus five squadrons of Dewoitine 520s—first-class planes in 1940—and five squadrons of Lioré-et-Olivier Le O 45s, which ultimately did a good job in Tunisia in 1943. At a pinch ten more squadrons could have been added, of reconnaissance Potez 63s and Bloch 175s, plus eleven other squadrons equipped with an assortment of other types. In all forty-six squadrons, manned by first-class crews who would have liked nothing better than to go fighting for France.

If only their chiefs had listened to de Gaulle, what an avalanche would have swept over the rear of the weak German and Italian forces in Libya, the Fezzan and Cyrenaica. It is easy to visualise what might have happened—the complete reversal of the situation, the repercussions in Greece and in Crete and even, in 1942, in the Far East. One thing is certain: the Germans would never, even with Franco's help, have been able to cross the Mediterranean. That excuse must be dismissed once and for all—that North Africa had to be safeguarded to prevent the Germans immediately seizing it! How could they have seized it? No, it won't do!

It took the Luftwaffe three months to recover from the Battle of France before it could start the attack on Britain.

Three out of every five of Rommel's supply ships were getting sunk in January 1941 by the two solitary torpedo-bomber squadrons based on Malta, and later in 1942 the proportion rose to nine out of ten.

Let us not forget that the entire merchant tonnage available in the Mediterranean would have been insufficient to transport six enemy divisions with full equipment and keep them supplied for a year. Furthermore, our French Navy, the quality of whose ships and crews excited the admiration of the whole world, was quite ready to fight alongside the Royal Navy. The Royal Navy in the Mediterranean, which kept the powerful Italian Navy at bay and trounced it regularly in every engagement, consisted merely of an old 1918 battleship, three cruisers and seven destroyers.

What a fine role France could have played!

Yes, I know that our ships had little A.A. and ammunition— enough all the same to fire on the Americans in 1942. I know, too, that our Air Force was short of spare parts for its planes. But something else I know is that we had some squadrons equipped with American planes, and that for three years the R.A.F. used Bostons, P-36s and Marylands earmarked for us and which even had French instrument panels. In 1940 these planes were in American docks, waiting for the word from us.

As for the squadrons equipped with French planes, they could have fought for a few months and kept going by cannibalisation. After all, how did American units manage in the Pacific in 1942? How did the South Africans manage for a whole year in the front line with their Junkers 86s? Does anyone suppose that the Luftwaffe sportingly supplied them with spare engines?

What about the Malta boys, who fought four against a hundred in Spitfires kept in the air by soldiers who learned about aircraft maintenance more or less as they went along? And what about the 3200 trucks handed over to Rommel, and captured when he was strangled by the R.A.F. at the end of 1942? Might they not have equipped French motorised units to fight the enemy, when Wavell had just about 500 vehicles to beat Graziani's forces in Libya?

Of course it would have made things tougher for the French in France, but so much was at stake—would it not have been worth it? Our moral fibre would have been in better shape in 1945, and we should have had even more right to our Allies' gratitude and respect.

It is precisely because of all this that men like Pijeaud got themselves killed, and that our comrades at Bir Hakeim were massacred to stop Rommel. Thanks to them, we could still hold our heads high.

This chapter is dedicated to Jean-Claude and Françoise Pijeaud. They know what the honour of France cost them.

* * *

Gambut, 20th December 1941

The Free French (Air Forces) 'Lorraine' bomber squadron was based at Gambut, a vast stretch of dust and stones in summer, a marsh in winter. The French shared it with a mixed British wing of Hurricanes and Blenheims.

All round the airfield the flying and ground personnel camped in extraordinary shanties knocked together out of empty cans, packing-cases and patched bits of tent-cloth. At night the cold was arctic, by day the sun roasted you. When it rained the men were devoured by insects and floundered in the mud, while the planes got bogged. After a couple of fine days you sank up to the ankles in a flour-like dust.

The men lived in conditions of hardship recalling those of medieval hermits and eastern slaves. Water was severely rationed and they had to fight the flies for the slice of corned beef which turned up regularly at every meal. The extremes of temperature, the lack of vitamins and chronic amoebic dysentery told on the crews. The infernal sand forced the fitters to work like slaves in hell. After thirty hours' flying-time an engine was worn out, the cylinders pitted, the valves eroded, and all the oil in the sumps got used up in a few hours. The salt damp rotted the cables inside their sheaths, the control-rods gave way and the oleos[8] seized up. Tyres had to be kept covered with moist cloths to prevent them bursting in the sun, and that made a big hole in the meagre water-ration. The petrol vapourised in the tanks, which burst at the joints—hence a constant risk of going up in flames in the air.

Taking off in a cloud of dust, which caked on the perspex charged with static, was an exhausting performance. The hot, dancing air, seemed unable to carry the planes and they would drop a wing at the slightest excuse. The superchargers vainly sucked in the warm rarefied air, and lost half their effectiveness.

---

[8] oleos = the legs of the undercarriage.

Sometimes a dust-storm rose on the horizon, veiling the sun. The opaque wall would hit the airfield at 60 m.p.h., smothering the men and equipment in a whirlwind of gritty sand. The sand penetrated everywhere, in your eyes, between your teeth, in the tool-kits, in the food, even in the petrol cans. It scraped the paint clean off the wings like emery paper.

When the elements let up, the Stukas and Junkers 88s would come along, bombing and strafing mercilessly. The tracer pierced the walls of the buildings and the splinters mowed down the men and set fire to the planes.

Sometimes, in the treacherous half-light after sunset, Messerschmitt 109s skimmed in over the dunes, zooming over the field like comets, their engines and guns roaring.

On top of that, there was the uncertainty of a fluid front. The men's nerves were strained to the limit by months of lightning attacks succeeded by disorderly retreats. The 'Lorraine' crews remembered how their mates in GC1, the Free French fighter squadron which had been left with their Hurricanes at Halfaya as rear-guard, had taken off under the fire of German tanks.

At night the slightest growl of an engine, the slightest sound of chains, reverberating in the silence of the desert, brought everybody immediately to their feet. It could be an enemy armoured column stabbing over the limitless plain.

A fortnight earlier Colonel Corniglion-Molinier had handed over as O.C. Lorraine Squadron to Colonel Pijeaud, who had previously been the first C.-in-C. of the F.F.A.F. in Great Britain and had come out to North Africa at his own wish. The twin-engined Blenheims of the French squadron each bore a large

Maltese, i.e. Lorraine, cross on the fuselage, to distinguish them from the British planes. The same proud emblem was embroidered on the shoulders of Koenig's men in the Free French Division which later defended Bir Hakeim, and of Leclerc's, whose column ranged over Tripolitania, as far as Tripoli itself.

The struggle had now entered a desperate phase. Rommel, who had just received thirty Mark IV tanks, was about to launch a new offensive towards Sidi Barrani, and all along the coast road enemy motorised and armoured columns were moving eastwards. Only air power could check the German offensive.

Every night the Wellingtons bombed Tripoli harbour. The Malta Beauforts harried the tankers in the Straits of Sicily and along the Libyan coast. The Hurricanes shot up the airstrips and escorted the day bombers.

This morning the Gambut wing was to attack a strong German-Italian column advancing on Barce. Eight Blenheims—four French, four British—were to take part in the show, escorted by sixteen Hurricanes from the same airfield. Colonel Pijeaud, in spite of his crews' advice, decided to lead the French Blenheims himself.

The meteorological forecast was not too good. 10/10th strato-cumulus at 5,000 feet made a uniform blanket over the whole coast, and above that, there were further layers of cloud up to 23,000 feet. It was an ideal set-up for an ambush by enemy fighters, and everybody was aware that a crack unit of the Luftwaffe, JG-18, had arrived on the front, equipped with Messerschmitt 109Fs and commanded by Marseille, one of the three great German aces.

Twice the operation was cancelled, and the crews nerves were all on edge. Even 'Papa' Masquelier's wise-cracks failed to raise a laugh.

Finally, just before midday, the O.K. came through. The Hurricanes took off first and did a wide orbit over the airfield to get into formation, and pick up the Blenheims taking off by fours through the blinding dust.

The formation had been flying for forty-five minutes, hard up against the cloud layer. On the right lay the blue sea, splashed with violet shadows from belts of cloud. Down below was the coast—Sollum bay with its huge overhanging cliff, Tobruk with its white houses scarred by traces of two sieges and its harbour choked with wreckage, and the crenellated pirates' stronghold of Jebel Akdar perched on its hill.

To the left the yellow desert, ploughed up by thousands of trucks and tanks, littered with burnt-out shells of vehicles, with here and there a clump of thorny bushes in the folds of a wadi. There was the railway, the line torn up by bombs, and the main Tobruk-Benghazi road.

The flak began to get aggressive and the formation was forced to climb through the clouds. The pilots were expecting a long spell of I.F., but they emerged into clear air within a few seconds. A warm current had carved a slice out of the upper layer and the planes found themselves flying between two uniform cloud layers. The Hurricanes closed in round the Blenheims, who had lost formation in the climb.

Colonel Pijeaud was clearly out of practice and handling his plane jerkily. The other three pilots found it hard to keep formation. The atmospheric conditions were rapidly deteriorating and the pilots looked around them with increasing anxiety.

The wing was now flying over Barce. Invisible to them, Major Marseille's Messerschmitts were taking off, 5,000 feet below the clouds. Ezanno, an old hand, who could smell trouble a mile off, sensed that all was not as it should be. His uneasiness spread to his crew. The English Wing-Co was running into a hornets' nest, but it was difficult for Pijeaud, on his first trip with the unit, to suggest they should turn back. Ezanno warned his crew over the inter-com to keep their eyes skinned, and also warned Pijeaud over the R/T to watch out for enemy fighters.

The formation veered to port towards Benina and the French 'box' moved across to let the British 'box' on its right slip under it. The four sections of the Hurricane escort were following very raggedly—probably something wrong with their R/T.

'Look out, chaps! One-o-Nines below!'

There they came, about forty Messerschmitts shooting up like arrows vertically out of the cloud layer below. They were the new Messerschmitt 109Fs with rounded wingtips. The Hurricanes hesitated for a moment, although it was clear from the peculiar camouflage that they were Jerries long before the black crosses could be made out.

Eight Hurricanes dived bravely to the attack, while the others came down lower to give closer protection to the bombers. Caught napping in the middle of a tricky 90-degree turn, the Franco-British formation had lost cohesion and was terribly vulnerable. It was too late to re-group as twelve more Messerschmitts emerged from the upper layer of cloud immediately above the Hurricanes of the close escort. They were trapped.

In a flash the sky was full of frantic planes firing or trying to break away, and already four Hurricanes in flames were plunging towards the sea. The British box tightened its left turn, hard pressed by the Messerschmitts. No. 3 Blenheim went into a spin, vomiting an enormous plume of spark-laden smoke.

Ezanno had immediately sized up the situation and shouted to Pijeaud to make for the shelter of the upper cloud-layer. But the other French Blenheims had made off after the three remaining British ones and were diving to catch them up, hoping that the cross-fire from their guns would keep the Germans off.

But they never got the chance, as the 109s attacked them at once. Flames from both engines enveloped Sergent-chef Redor's plane, licking the ailerons. Two Messerschmitts went for him, and his Blenheim, now beyond control, slipped sideways, then went over on its back and vanished.

The Wing-Co had had it. No. 4 was out of control and its crew baling out. No. 2, with its bombs on board, went off like a grenade, less than twenty-five yards from Ezanno.

Charbonneau and Ezanno tried to cover Pijeaud, who was in difficulties. His dead gunner had collapsed inside the transparent dorsal turret and his punctured tanks were pouring out two thick trails of white petrol vapour. The colonel ordered his navigator to jump, and the white mushroom shape went floating down amidst the dog-fights between the Messerschmitts and the Hurricanes. The British fighters, outnumbered five to one, just hadn't a chance.

There seemed no point in staying on. The two Blenheims' only chance was to make for the clouds, each on its own. Ezanno pulled away from Charbonneau, did a split-arse turn then climbed flat out, followed by four 109s. The Messerschmitts, their lines sharpened by the speed, looked like adders. With their yellow noses and rust-brown and yellow camouflage, spotted with green, they spiralled round the Blenheim in a deadly dance, drawing gradually closer, their cannon roaring and their tracer striating the sky.

His teeth gritted and his breath coming in gasps Ezanno hurled his plane into the wildest manoeuvres to try and throw the enemy off. He half turned on his back then violently straightened out again. Tournier, desperately trying to find something to hold on to, was hurled to and fro against the sides of the cockpit. Baudin, his face smarting from burning powder and choking from the smoking grease in his overheating machine-guns, went on firing away at the Messerschmitts, now attacking at point-blank range.

Every enemy shell that went home shook the Blenheim, whose airframe was groaning under the strain of so much turning at speed. Air whistled through the shell-holes and tore off strips of aluminium loosened by the explosions.

Very gradually, thanks to the skill of its pilot and its manoeuvrability, the Blenheim succeeded in gaining height. The German section-leader, recognisable by his yellow spinner and the white-edged chevrons painted on his fuselage, realised what the Blenheim was up to and tried to cut him off. He made a wide circle round the bomber as the other Messerschmitts hemmed it in and then made a daring attack at it from about 2 o'clock. Ezanno immediately put all his weight on the rudder-bar, heaved the plane round to face him, firing with his fixed machine-guns. The 109, who was already coming in, waggled his wings and then skidded away, but not before catching a packet— a plate came off his wing, followed by some fragments. But he too had been on the mark—and a 20-mm. shell smashed a switch panel behind Tournier's head, as he sat helpless in his transparent cage.

'He's yours, Baudin, get him as he comes past!'

The Messerschmitt skimmed by the Blenheim, but ran into a hail of bullets from the turret. There was a thread of smoke, a slender flame between the radiators. The Messerschmitt went over on its back, the perspex hood flew off and the hunched-up figure of the pilot was seen to jump clear.

The way was now clear and Ezanno[9] thankfully disappeared into the clouds.

* * *

From the ditch where they had prudently retired, two Italian truck-drivers suddenly saw a plane emerge from the grey clouds, its cockpit in flames.

It was Pijeaud. The petrol ducts under the seat had burst and, one hand still gripping the stick, he sheltered his eyes from the

---

[9] Colonel Ezanno, probably the best all-round French pilot of the Second World War, was at the time of writing Inspector of Fighter Aircraft with the French Air Ministry.

flames with the other. In spite of the fearful pain, he had managed to keep his aircraft level long enough to give his crew a chance to bale out. He had seen the navigator jump, but he was not sure about the gunner. Too late now, he was too low. All he could do was try and belly-land his plane on the road.

Blinded by the roaring flames, choked by the smoke, he went on flying by instinct. The perspex was all gone and the inrush of air was turning the whole cabin into a furnace. There was a scream of tearing metal, a shower of sparks, debris and stones, and the Blenheim skidded to a halt on its belly in a cloud of dust. A shape emerged from the blazing wreckage, staggered a few steps and collapsed.

The two Italians came rushing up. At last, a prisoner! They hauled the man to his feet and bundled him into the back of their truck, in spite of his lacerated face and hands. Colonel Pijeaud, for it was he, fainted away.

The truck turned and set off back for Benghazi. On the way it was hailed by a German pilot sitting on the bank and cluttered up with his hastily folded parachute. It was the officer shot down by Baudin and Ezanno. From his refined features and the Iron Cross with Swords and Oak-leaves, the Italian driver had no difficulty in recognising Major Marseille, the Afrika Korps ace, credited with eighty successes.

Captain Ezanno, after stooging around in the clouds for ten minutes to get back his wind and to put the enemy off the scent, came down to ground-level again to look for the enemy arm-oured column, the object of the trip. He followed the coast road right up to Apollonia without finding it. On the way he shot up a few isolated M/T and himself got shot at by some flak. Then he came across two Hurricanes, the sole survivors of the escort. The Blenheim led them back, 'on the deck' all the way, jumping obstacles and sneaking through the wadis, as far as their home base at Bu Amud, then returned to Gambut to land.

Charbonneau was back, and the bad news had already got around. An anxious crowd was waiting for Ezanno, to hear what more he knew.

The fitters who checked his Blenheim found nearly sixty bullet and shell hits. One aileron wire was severed, and there were bits of Messerschmitt 109 wedged between the cylinders of the starboard engine.

Out of twenty-four planes that had set out, only four came back—the two Hurricanes and the two bombers with the Lorraine crosses.

Colonel Pijeaud escaped with two British officers from Dema hospital three days later, in spite of appalling burns and his being still more or less blind. They walked for four nights without food or water, lying up among rocks along the coast in the daytime.

Eventually an Australian recce column picked them up, collapsed in the bottom of a dried-up water-hole. In spite of dreadful pain, Pijeaud was still alive. He had the strength of will to dictate his op. report while the medical orderlies bound up his wounds.

For nine days his martyrdom went on, on board a hospital ship. On 6th January 1942 he died.

Almost two years later, on 13th December 1943, Colette

Pijeaud, his heroic wife who had been deported by the Germans, died of whip-lashes at Ravensbrück, leaving two orphans to bear that great name—Jean-Claude, thirteen years old, and Francoise, eleven.

CHAPTER SIX

FLAMES OVER WARSAW

'Lord God Almighty, the children of a warlike nation raise to Thee their disarmed hands. They call to Thee from the depths of the mines of Siberia and of the snows of Kamchatka. From Muscovite and Prussian servitude, Oh Lord, deliver us.'

From a poem of 1831 by ADAM MICKIEWICZ.

AT 8.15 a.m. on the 29th July 1944, Radio-Moscow broadcast in Polish the following call to the Resistance in Warsaw:

'For Warsaw, which has never given in and has continued to fight, the hour of action has come.

'The Germans will doubtless try and make a stand in the city, piling up more ruins and massacring thousands more victims. Your houses and gardens, your bridges and stations, your factory and office buildings will be turned into defensive positions by the enemy. They will expose the city to destruction and its inhabitants to certain death. They will pillage, and reduce to dust what they cannot take away.

'That is why it is more than ever necessary to remember that the Hitlerite flood destroys everything. Only an active effort, and fighting in the streets, the houses, the factories and the shops of Warsaw will bring nearer the hour of liberation and save both the town's heritage and the fives of your fellow citizens.

'Poles, the hour of liberation is at hand!

'Poles, to arms!

'Do not lose an instant, Praga and the industrial suburbs of Warsaw are already within range of Russian guns!'

At 5 p.m. on 1st August, a bomb went off in the Gestapo Headquarters, which unleashed the insurrection. 50,000 soldiers of the Polish underground army, helped by the entire population, seized three-quarters of the city after five hours' bitter fighting which cost them more than 7000 killed.

The trap was set, and, in full view of the whole civilised world, was about to close mercilessly on the Polish martyrs.

As soon as the insurrection was really under way the Soviet troops withdrew six miles under orders from Moscow, thus breaking off contact with the Germans, though they were in full retreat. Rokossovsky was to remain a neutral but interested spectator, while the S.S. wiped out all those embarrassing patriots.

The Polish Prime Minister, Mikolajczyk, at once took a plane to Moscow, to try to move Stalin. Stalin replied that he would help Warsaw only on condition that Poland accepted the Lublin puppet government and also the Curzon Line.

Mikolajczyk sent a heart-rending appeal to Roosevelt, who intervened on 24th August. Stalin did not even reply to the Anglo-American request for the use of airfields to enable the R.A.F. and the U.S.A.F. to bring supplies to Warsaw by air. In the meantime the Soviet radio was claiming that 'reactionary elements in Warsaw had risen without orders, to sabotage the operations of the victorious Red Army.'

The Russian refusal over the airfields was particularly surprising as, three months earlier, on seven separate occasions, American forces of 500 to 700 bombers and fighters from England had landed on Russian territory after raids on East Prussia. These planes had then left for North Africa, after being refueled by the Russians, bombing on their way targets in Austria and Czechoslovakia.

On his own initiative, Churchill then authorised the Special Services of the R.A.F. to try and keep Warsaw supplied whatever the risk. Very few aircraft were available at that time, as by and large the whole of Transport Command was fully occupied keeping the Allied Armies supplied in their dash for the Rhine. The units that did try lost 85 per cent, of their planes in six nights and Air-Marshal Slessor regretfully had to put a stop to these suicide trips.

The only units that were able to go on were the Polish Special Duties units and also two South African squadrons in the Middle East, who enjoyed a relatively independent status.

It was appalling. In two months 138 Special Duties Squadron (Polish) lost sixty-five officers and one hundred and sixty-nine other ranks, i.e. thirty-two crews and planes. These incredible losses were sustained over twenty-three nights and represented 90 per cent, of the aircraft sent. In six weeks the South Africans lost twenty-four out of their thirty-three Liberators.

Although he was fifty-four years old, General Raisky, C.-in-C.

of the Polish Air Force in 1939, flew a Halifax himself on three of the trips.

What made it all still more heart-rending was that the enormous distance to be covered prevented more than quite a small cargo being taken. In the event only about, forty tons of arms and ammunition, etc., reached the resistance forces in Warsaw.

As Roosevelt refused to intervene more energetically, Churchill sent a very violently worded message to Stalin, who eventually replied on 10th September (forty days after the rising in Warsaw had begun) that Poltawa airfield would be available for American planes on two days only, 16th and 17th September.

Churchill, completely disgusted, declared: 'Stalin has summarily rejected our proposals. I could hardly believe my eyes when I read his cruel reply. I was so angry that I told Roosevelt he should give orders that American planes must land on Russian bases by force. Stalin would never have dared fire on them.' But Roosevelt kept on insisting that his friend Stalin might be brutal, but he was sincere, and that retaining his friendship was more important than those Poles.

In the meantime the Germans were free to launch eight divisions against Warsaw, burning and destroying the whole town and massacring its inhabitants. For sixty-three days, General Bor-Komorovski and his men covered themselves with glory, defending Warsaw foot by foot and house by house.

In the end, on 2nd October 1944, abandoned by all her Allies[10]

---

[10] Except France. Let it be remembered to her honour, de Gaulle had two very heated discussions with Stalin on the subject of Warsaw and did not budge an inch.

and sacrificed by Roosevelt on the altar of Stalin's friendship, Warsaw, razed to the ground, capitulated. 200,000 of its inhabitants were dead, the surviving 350,000 were deported to Germany.

At 8 p.m. on 1st October Warsaw radio made its last broadcast : 'This is the bitter truth—we have been treated worse than Hitler's satellites; worse than Italy, worse than Rumania, worse than Finland God is righteous, and in His omnipotence He will punish all those responsible for this terrible injury to the Polish nation.'

Surviving comrades of the Polish Air Forces, whose proud device was 'Destiny can wait', and who are now scattered in exile in every corner of the world, it is to you that I dedicate this story of the operational flight carried out by 138 SD Squadron on 6th September 1944.

Brindisi, 6th September 1944

The six Halifaxes of the Polish 138 'Special Duties' Squadron took off in turn from the Italian airfield and lumbered away, painfully getting up to their safe flying-speed[11] over the harbour.

It was 7 o'clock. The golden sunlight was softly gathered in the falling summer day and in the diaphanous cirrus clouds. It was the hour when, now that the war had receded to the North, the calm sea and the warm air breathed the joy of living.

The Halifaxes were heavily laden; petrol for twelve hours' flying and three tons of arms and ammunition in parachute

---

[11] Safe flying-speed is the minimum speed at which a plane can fly and turn if one of its engines packs up.

containers. The engines were labouring, flat out, the pilots climbing as steeply as they could without stalling, for the Adriatic is narrow and Yugoslavia's tall mountains already capped the horizon. They also had to gain height quickly because in the Mediterranean the period of twilight is long and night hesitates before finally falling—and the Messerschmitt 109s stood guard on their Dalmatian airfields.

The Halifax flown by F/Lt. R. Chmiel, bearing the chequered red-and-white insignia of the Polish Air Force, crossed the Balkan coast at Dubrovnik.

Night had now swallowed up the mountains of Serbia. Hundreds of partisan fires twinkled amongst the hills, and lower down, in the valleys, the S.S. patrols had theirs too. The moon rose over the Alps and the pale Austrian plain, where the Danube, like a silvery ribbon, trailed its hundred loops. Vienna was over there to the left, invisible.

Everything was O.K. on board. The crew were silent, but they were thrilled to be making for Poland, their own country. The compass showed their course set for Warsaw. Theirs was a desperate mission, to help the desperate defenders of that heroic city.

Beneath the aircraft the plain began to wrinkle, to heave. Soon the mountains of the High Tatra appeared, their summits sprinkled with early snow. The moon had disappeared, blotted out by a dense cloud front which billowed in low dark rolling waves.

And there was Poland; but with the moonshine everything else had gone too; the big shining lakes, the forests, the white quarries were all hidden in the gloom. The crew's long agony was beginning.

They were beginning to feel the first onset of fatigue, after flying for five long hours. The heavy four-engined planes ploughed their way through the treacherous storm-laden clouds. All along their track the flak opened up, the brief flashes from the 88-mm. visible in the valleys, on the hills and along the roads. One would have imagined that the planes were sprinkling the earth with stars as they passed over.

'Navigator to pilot. Searchlights and flak three o'clock, some way off.'

Every face turned. A dozen or so miles away another Halifax was transfixed by the rapiers of the searchlights and all around flak was bursting. Then suddenly everything went dark, except for one drunken comet which spiralled quickly down and then vanished. Only five Halifaxes now.

After that the night seemed darker and thicker still. The pilots had to turn the instrument-panel lighting as low as possible, but it still seemed blindingly bright. Hours of inky blackness, all alike in that tunnel of cloud.

Then suddenly the horizon seemed hollowed out and reddened like the dawn. Drops of blood seemed to form on the frosty perspex.

The planes began to lose height—6000 feet . . . 5000 feet—and the speed increased. The source of the glow was hidden behind the black earth, but it gradually filled the sky. A vivid scarlet snake twisted under the wings—it was the Vistula; and, like a brilliant sunrise, Warsaw in flames was before them. The crews, hypnotised, drank in the light. The wireless operator had half risen to his feet and was looking over the pilot's shoulder. The machine-gunners had turned their turrets to face forwards. Only the rear gunner, tucked away at the other end of the long fuselage between the two fins, looked out into the night and saw nothing— but his heart told him his country's capital was there.

The vast brazier, devouring thousands upon thousands of burning, collapsing houses, lit the sky and showed up the dark outlines of the Halifaxes. From as far out as Sluzew flak ringed the town, and, at the sound of the engines, the 88s stopped firing horizontally over the town and began to grope the sky.

The town was one vast inferno, the ground and the sky mingling in one blinding eruption of flame. And men had been fighting in that hell for thirty-eight days already.

The aircraft came down low over the river to avoid the flak and jumped the wrecked bridges, whose shattered piles were mirrored in the blood-stained water. The pilot felt he was piercing a thick wall of fire. The engine temperatures shot up and the acrid smoke invaded the Halifax, making the crew cough.

Suddenly they entered a patch of shadow. It was the western part of the town, held by the enemy and where the insurrection had been quelled early on.

Only a few isolated groups of partisans still held out there, surrounded by the S.S. troops. Searchlights were trained along the avenues lighting up the fronts of the houses. At every street corner there was a multiple pom-pom spraying the roofs with explosive bullets and covering the hesitant advance of the tanks.

A South-African Liberator came skimming over the chimney-stacks, firing with all its guns. It shot out some of the searchlights, but then the pilot, probably dazzled, crashed into a church steeple.

Further on the furnace began again. How could the charred debris of a town still continue to throw up so much heat and flame? How could General Bor's men, hammered by German artillery, survive in this brazier—not only survive, but fight?

Even the drains were ablaze. The Germans had expended valuable reserves of fuel in an attempt to dislodge the partisans from the underground labyrinth that the S.S. patrols dare not venture into.

Warsaw presented such an appalling sight that the men in the Halifax wept, the tears leaving glistening traces as the heat dried them on their soot-blackened faces. They wept for their rent country, the monstrous war, their enemies' ruthlessness, their Allies' treachery and cowardice. They wept for their families buried alive in their homes. They wept for the futility of their own share in the fight now, and for a life without the savour of hope.

Over to the right the outline of a crippled Halifax appeared for a second against the wall of light and then fell into the conflagration—an incandescent spark falling back into the forest fire.

Like converging spokes of a wheel the Tiger tanks, crushing the debris under their tracks, were slowly working their way towards the burning centre of the old town, the headquarters of the Resistance. Chmiel saw two of them edging through the rubble and waving their long gun like the trunk of some pre-historic monster. The rear-gunner fired a long burst with his four Brownings, but the tracer bounced off the armour-plating like drops of water off a lump of granite. Suddenly one of the

Tigers disappeared under an avalanche of rubble as a cellar roof collapsed under it. The Halifax circled over the flames at 300 m.p.h. The paint blistered on the wings and the showers of sparks eroded the perspex, making it opaque.

Trying to find the flares marking the Dropping Zone in this blinding chaos was obviously useless, and even the navigator from his vantage point in the bomb-aimer's transparent blister could not make out the streets of his native town amongst those heaps of rubble. Microphone in hand, he tried to guide his pilot.

Other aircraft were braving the storm and struggling to get to the centre of the conflagration. Four Liberators of the South African S.A.S. Squadron had come on the suicide trip out of loyalty to their Polish comrades. Blinded, flaps down, they were stooging round, trying to find where they could drop their precious containers. The flak pursued them relentlessly, and, one by one, the big planes went down.

Chmiel's navigator kept on trying, but it was difficult. Streets? What streets? Where were they in that nightmarish moonscape where the ground itself seemed to burn and vitrify the rubble to a level flatness?

They must find the Dropping Zone fast, drop the arms and ammunition and then get away from this flaming vault.

Ashes fell like black snow, but never reached the ground. They remained suspended between earth and sky as new gusts of hot air belched forth by the boiling cauldron below swirled them up afresh thousands of feet into the air.

The crew of the Halifax were drugged with horror. There comes a point where despair drives out fear, and those seven men felt that their taut nerves had passed beyond even that point, into a state where nothing was left but hate and a desire for sacrifice. The normal regular laws of nature were in abeyance, and F/Lt. Chmiel knew that if he said the word the whole crew was ready to hurl itself at the enemy and crash the plane on a Hun target.

Ah! here was the district round the railway station, recaptured by the Hermann Goering Division. They could see a pontoon-bridge, hastily thrown over the Vistula by the Germans—the bridges in the city centre were all controlled by the insurgents—and a German convoy crossing. The trucks were bumper to bumper, and among the mass of vehicles on the embankment there five big self-propelled guns. The Germans, having nothing to fear from the Russian Air Force for the time being, were taken by surprise.

The turrets of the Halifax spat fire, the automatic 20-mm. on the ground replied angrily.

'If only, if only we had some bombs!' The pilot gritted his teeth and fought the crazy temptation of turning about and crushing the whole set-up under the Halifax's thirty-ton weight. No! he must first deliver the Sten guns, the Brens and the grenades to Bor-Komorovski's soldiers, who needed them so desperately. And he must also get back to his base, to be able to return the next day, and go on returning until the flak finally got him.

'Navigator to pilot. This is Poniatovski Bridge, turn right at the next one.'

Here was the old town again, flanked by the working-class districts. The blackened skeletons of the blocks of flats rising from the shambles. Over Kierbedz Bridge the plane turned and found itself over Krasinski Square. Five green flares in the shape of a cross and sheets arranged in a T-shape to show the direction of the wind—as if every flame for miles around didn't already sufficiently show that!—it was the D.Z.

Men were running below, waving. The Halifax turned tight, flaps down, engines throttled back, and came back over the square, bomb-bays open. Just then black puffs appeared over the ruined buildings—it was the 88s on the hill in the park shooting at the plane. The splinters mowed down some of the men on the ground, and, just as the containers fell clear, the Halifax was shaken by a terrific explosion. It was almost turned on its back, but the pilot miraculously righted it, so low that it hit a wall—No. 4 engine started racing, its propeller had gone west. The flight engineer, his stomach ripped open by a splinter, raised himself on his arms, switched the engine off and closed the fuel-cock.

The parachutes hardly slowed down the fall of the dangling cylinders in that superheated air. Three of them caught fire before reaching the ground.

In the aircraft Chmiel wrestled with the controls. Round him the wounded moaned—four of the crew had been hit by the shrapnel which had riddled the fuselage. The navigator, hurled across the cabin by the explosion, had smashed his skull on a corner of the radio set and a trickle of blood flowed from his nose. He was cluttering up the gangway.

'Task completed! We must get out of this.' Straight back was out of the question, as every flak battery was on the *qui vive*.

They would have to skirt north-east and north of Warsaw and find shelter in the shadows on the right bank of the Vistula. There stood Rokossovsky's troops, thirty divisions halted in their headlong pursuit of the Germans by order of the Kremlin, and now calmly waiting for the tragedy to run its course.

The crew of the Halifax were exhausted, but they still had six hours' flying time ahead of them—probably seven, on three engines—before they could get the wounded back to Brindisi. It was pretty rough, when there were Allied airfields a few minutes away. Allied? The pilot shrugged his shoulders and turned left to get on to a southerly course.

'Look out, pilot! Plane seven o'clock! '

Chmiel, in spite of being an engine short, started to corkscrew. Down to pick up speed, then up and away to the right. The string of tracer passed under the wing and went weaving away into the night.

Where was that plane now? He was certainly coming back, as the Halifax was a perfect target, outlined against the burning city. The night-fighter, painted black against the black sky, its exhausts carefully masked, slipped through the night, keeping his target between the glare and himself.

'There he is!'

The pedal-operated turret swivelled round and the mid-upper gunner had his hand on the button ready to fire, when an extra large explosion over there in Warsaw raised the veil for an instant and revealed the enemy plane.

It was a low-wing twin-engined plane with a glass-house nose and twin fins.

'Holy Mother of God!'

Its fuselage bore a red star.

'Hullo, mid-upper, can you still see him?'

No reply.

'Well, can you? Answer!'

In the end a voice stammered in the intercom. 'I didn't shoot. . . . I couldn't. . . . It was a Pe-2.'

But the Pe-2 had shot all right.

The Halifax set course for Brindisi again. The rear-gunner, numb with cold in his turret, was not the last to see the bloody light over Warsaw, which was destined to continue for twenty-six days and twenty-six nights more. They could not call up the other planes in 138 Squadron over the R/T as they still had five hours' flying over enemy territory—long, anxious hours.

Just as the radiant summer sun rose over Italy the Halifax at last landed on Brindisi airfield. The other pilots were anxiously waiting for her, together with the ambulance and the fire-crew.

As he taxied towards the control tower Chmiel instinctively counted the empty dispersal bays. The five other planes must be lost; they could not be behind him, as he was late himself and his tanks were empty.

He cleared and switched off his last engine. The medical orderlies took off the wounded. The rest of the crew jumped down.

How blue the sky was here! When their mates ran up and asked how it had been, they shook their heads and said nothing. They had not yet emerged from their nightmare.

CHAPTER SEVEN

MAX GUEDJ

The Mess in the Free French Air Forces H.Q. in South Kensington, 25th August 1944.

At a corner of the bar he sat silent and alone, for he was not of a 'matey' disposition and his recent experiences had embittered him. We were at the other end of the room talking in low voices, and about him, naturally. Through all our talk about 'shop' you could sense our intense admiration for Max, the famous Squadron-Leader 'Maurice' of Coastal Command, and we were not exactly beginners ourselves.

On his uniform he wore the Croix de la Liberation, the D.S.O. and a double D.F.C. Max Guedj already had more than a hundred shipping strikes in Beau-fighters and Mosquitos to his credit. He commanded a wing. He was surrounded for us young chaps by a halo of respect, even of legend—the *Prinz Eugen* do on 12th May 1942, the two Junkers 88s shot down off Royan after a dog-fight which lasted a full forty minutes, the Brest show, etc, etc. It all served to isolate him even more.

We knew from the B.B.C. that a couple of days previously he had led fifteen Mosquitoes in an attack on two mine-sweepers and a Narvik class destroyer near Le Verdon, and that the mine-sweepers had been sunk by rocket fire and the destroyer severely damaged. We also knew that he had every reason to be sad, for he had had to leave his baby daughter behind in Morocco, and he knew that his father had been clapped in prison by Frenchmen in the service of the Germans.

What always surprised us was his preference for shipping strikes. Hardly what one would expect of a man of thirty-two with a cool clear brain and a legal training. He was at the head of one of those units made up of real hard cases, few of whom survived a whole tour of operations of thirty trips. For three and a half years he had been holding out in a branch of the service where 75 per cent losses in one month was normal.

For one thing, the flak was frightful. On the previous day, for example, 24th August, twelve Beaufighters from 236 Squadron and eight from 404, led by E. W. Tacon, a New Zealander, had attacked the two destroyers stationed at the Pointe de Graves. The two ships had sunk in flames, but only three Beaus had got back.

The enemy fighters were worse still. In the previous March, for instance, six Messerschmitt 109s from Mérignac had jumped six Torbeaus (Torpedo-Beaufighters), only two of which got away, and one of those killed its crew when it crashed on landing.

It was 12.30. The Colonel and the staff officers got up. Lunch was ready. We watched Max get up too, and go with them. We never saw him again. The pace of the air war was getting hotter, and Max seldom took his statutory leave.

On a dreary winter's day in 1945 Jacques Remlinger and I were sitting in Pete Wickham's office at Fighter Command H.Q.

at Stanmore. A telegram arrived and he handed it to me without a word. Jacques read over my shoulder, 'Max missing.'

We were flabbergasted. It was incredible. Max, the greatest ace in the whole French Air Force from 1939 to 1945, to get himself shot down in Norway, after four years of fighting, with France already liberated and the war nearly over! And yet, in one sense, what an admirable end—to go off like that, away from the sun, into the cold shadow of the Arctic Circle, the cinders of his body scattered over the icy waters, of Ofot Fjord.

R.A.F. Coasted Fighter Station, Banff

He stepped out of the darkness and silence of the deserted airfield into the light of the Mess. The two blankets slung across the door fell back behind him. He blinked as he took off his Irvine jacket, the collar of which was damp with fog and smelt of mutton fat and crudely tanned leather. The air was full of the noise of chairs falling and furniture being knocked about. The sinking of a 9000-ton transport at the entrance of the Zuyder Zee was being celebrated and the chaps were having a wizard time.

Max stopped by the door for a moment, slipping his forage cap under his shoulder strap with the old familiar gesture. His entry was greeted as usual with cries of 'Good evening, Sir. Have a drink, Sir?'

'No, thank you.' He was always conscious of his sharp voice and of his French accent.

The party was going with a swing. They had the S/Ldr. Admin. cornered in the angle of the bar, and while four pilots were holding on to his arms and legs, a fifth, egged on by the excited onlookers, was setting fire to his tie with a cigarette lighter.

They're all completely mad, thought Max. There were Canadians present, Australians, about thirty British, two Americans, a Belgian and some New Zealanders, all kids of eighteen to twenty-five, and all under his orders.

'Maurice, it will be a tough job,' had said Air-Marshal Slessor, A.O.C. Coastal Command, when he had entrusted him with the Wing. Being French made it no easier: he was hard on his crews, too, though no harder than on himself. At bottom they respected him, which was their way of feeling affection. They respected him for his D.S.O., and particularly because they knew he was the best among them—the first to dive through the flak, the best shot, the best pilot. It was professional respect, perhaps the finest form of affection that a pilot can show.

Max looked at his watch. 10 p.m.—time to close down.

'All right, chaps, bed now.'

His voice was audible above the tumult, which died down gradually. Only those who had had one or two over the eight went on talking just the same. That sort of moment is difficult for anyone in command, the atmosphere of the Mess is so friendly and intimate.

'Strike laid on at dawn,' he added in the same tone of voice, so that it shouldn't sound like an apology. That did it. Everybody drank up and filed out in twos, crew by crew, into the hall. Max was already in his room at the end of the corridor, a room in the Mess itself being the privilege of a unit commander.

A quarter of an hour later the streaks of light under the Nissen hut doors disappeared one by one. The station was asleep. Only the intermittent flashing of the beacon from the control tower indefatigably cut up the night.

0530 hours

F/Lt. Forbes, I.O. on night duty, woke up with a start. The bell of the teletype had gone off and the rustle of the paper unrolling and the clack-clack of the machine-gun had begun.

In a corner of the Ops. Room the duty sergeant jumped out of his camp bed as the mercury-vapour lamps began to flicker, and took up his position by the telephone. A glance at the paper unrolling: '*Operation Number 005718 stop Priority top secret stop all available aircraft shipping strike Ofot Fjord H hour . . .*'

From now on it was the well-known drill which the duty officer knew backwards without having to check up on the list of instructions hanging by the Tannoy mike—Wake Wing Commander flying; alert station armament and engineer officers, alert navigation officer and senior I.O.; get word to officers, sergeants and airmen's Messes; alert S.Ps. and guard-room; all passes to be suspended till take-off; phone communications to the town to be cut.

The 1200 men of the base were jerked awake by the strident sound of the loudspeaker hanging at every corner. The well-oiled machine smoothly slipped into gear.

Before it ever got to the teletype stage Operation Order CC1.005718 Form D had already covered a lot of ground.

On the previous evening the Strat-R Spitfire XI had landed at

Peterhead after a 1200-mile trip over the North Sea as far as Tromso in Norway, well inside the Arctic Circle. The pilot, exhausted by four hours' flying in storms, had had to be helped out of his cockpit, while fitters got the frozen cameras loose with jets of steam.

The developed photos had shown a naval convoy entering Ofot Fjord—a 6000-ton tanker escorted by a big Elbing class destroyer, two Sans-Souci class escort vessels and two Flak-ships, including an ice-breaker. While Max's crews were having a high old time bringing the roof down in the Mess, a conference was being held 200 miles away in the Coastal Command 19 Group H.Q.

Air-Marshal Sir Brian Baker and Air-Marshal Frank Linden Hopps, A.O.C. Strike Group, after hearing the Intelligence and Navy reports on the importance of the target, had decided to detail for the job the Mosquitoes of 143, 235 and 248 Squadrons commanded by Wing-Commander Maurice.

The American Liaison Officer had immediately got through to 66th Fighter-Wing, 8th U.S. Air Force, at Sawston, to find out what they would be able to spare for escort duties. A call to the Uxbridge H.Q. of A.D.G.B. provisionally earmarked 315 Polish Squadron. This was a Mustang unit and had plenty of experience of escorts over Norway.

The Liaison Officers notified A.A. Command and the Royal Navy of the probable time-table and route of the aircraft, in order to avoid unfortunate misunderstandings.

Everything had been discussed and arranged in a calm, matter-of-fact way, just as if it had been a commercial enterprise being launched. The outcome of all this preliminary work was the Form D now coming through on all the teletypes.

While Max was getting dressed—R.A.F. wool and silk under-clothes, pullover, leather jerkin under the battle-dress blouse, long woollen stockings inside the lined boots—the whole station had become furiously active.

Tractors brought up trailers bearing the long heavy semi-armour-piercing explosive rockets, each weighing sixty pounds. The armourers fitted into the tails of the rockets cruciform cordite charges, which would propel them at 1000 feet per second. They then carefully screwed on over the platinum plate of the electric detonator and the firing contacts the fins designed to stabilise the rockets in flight.

The Mosquito 6's Rolls-Royce 'Merlin 25' engines were started up, warmed and run up by the fitters. The big bowser (truck) passed from plane to plane making sure that every one of the ten separate tanks in each aircraft was topped up, making a total load of 500 gallons. As part of the routine drill, the riggers checked the oxygen bottles—actually they would not be needed as it was going to be the usual low-level trip.

In the cookhouses the W.A.A.F. personnel were preparing porridge and eggs and bacon for the forty pilots and observers who were going on the show.

In the quiet of the Ops. Room F/Lt. Forbes and the Senior Intelligence Officer made sure that each crew's wallet contained a complete set of maps, charts and photos. Standing on a ladder, the sergeant was fixing ribbons on the wall map from

Sumburgh to Narvik, blue for the Mosquitoes' route and white for the escort fighters. Bent over a table covered with graduated rulers and protractors, F/Lt. Langley, navigation leader for the strike, was working out his courses E.T.As. and then chalking them up on the blackboard. Next to the board was a screen on which in a few minutes' time the projector would show photos of Ofot Fjord and the latest ones of the convoy, brought at that very moment by a frozen and mud-bespattered despatch rider from Group.

0830 hours

The crews were all assembled in the briefing room. No sign of yesterday's youthful high spirits in the intent faces to be seen there now—they seemed ageless, like the faces of men who were going to face death. In a few months a mask as of ten extra years had been impressed on their young features; their own mothers sometimes did not recognise them, when they survived to go home.

Everyone looked at the board, where the blue ribbon ended in Narvik, in the centre of a large red blotch—extra-heavy flak zone. In the Senior I.O's. office Max was on the phone with Air-Marshal Hoops—'Hoppy' to his pilots—who had wanted to give him his final instructions in person. The pilots strained their ears, but all they got was 'Yes, Sir . . . yes, Sir.'

Now silence fell as Max went up on the platform. He was used to this ceremony by now, but every time he slowly walked up those steps he felt he was jumping over a wall into another world.

Three more trips and he would go on leave, requested to do so by his own chiefs and by General de Gaulle.

'Attention, please. Eighteen Mosquitoes plus one reserve from 143, 235 and 248 Squadrons are to attack and destroy a 6000-ton tanker moored at the head of Romback Fjord.

'Romback Fjord is a continuation inland of Ofot or Narvik Fjord, which some of you are pretty well acquainted with already. As the distances involved are bigger than our normal maximum and as we are taking a full load of rockets, we shall put down in Sumburgh in the Shetlands to refuel on the way.

'The A.O.C. has just told me over the phone what extreme importance is attached in the highest quarters to the destruction of this ship. It is carrying high octane aviation spirit for the German airfields in Northern Norway, of which, as you know, there are twelve important ones between Bodö and Tromsö. The German evacuation plan involves the transfer north of a large part of the very strong forces the Luftwaffe still has in Denmark. If they succeed it may mean two months added on to the war, and make necessary a large-scale amphibious operation to liberate Norway, which would mean more casualties, lots of them.

'It's going to be a tricky job. The Torbeaus refused to take it on, because Romback Fjord is too narrow for them, and these days they don't believe torpedoes can be relied on when there is ice in the water. The *Nuremberg* show in '42 showed they're right. Do you remember? She was caught in the ice off North Cape and made an ideal target. But all the torpedoes exploded against ice floes, and all that happened was we lost four Torbeaus. Jerry must have been laughing like a drain!

144

'We are the only unit fast enough to go up the forty miles of Narvik Fjord without too much unpleasantness with the flak—we hope!

'The met. forecast isn't too good. There will be snow and icing. On the other hand, it may put off the Focke-Wulf 190s at Bardufoss and Skaaland.

'Our fighter escort will go direct from Peterhead to the rendezvous over the sea. It'll be the Mustangs of 135 Polish Squadron.

'We'll fly in battle formation, sections of three and four, line abreast. Don't straggle, otherwise you'll certainly lose contact in this lousy visibility. The two reserves will kindly not try to be too funny. Their job is to come with the rest of us until we pick up the fighters and then take over from anyone who is in difficulties, if there is anyone. Absolute R/T silence, of course, only visual signals to be used.

'When we get to the objective, Revolver will attack first, then Shark, but only if the target is not yet destroyed. Blue Sections from Revolver and Shark will form a separate section which will take on the flak ships.

'Aim at the base of the funnels at 300 yards, don't dive too steeply, and your rockets will strike at the water line.

'If enemy fighters attack, form a defensive circle, reduce speed, 10 degrees of flap and keep turning. If you are alone, there's only one sensible thing to do—full throttle, make for the clouds, not forgetting, of course, to use your cannon if the opportunity arises.

'Every observer will keep an individual navigation log, so that he can get home on his own if he has to.

'Any questions? All right, that's all. Good hunting!'

For the perfect execution of a shipping strike it is necessary to get all the aircraft away together and form up immediately as a group. A tricky business with Mosquitoes, as they overheat very quickly when taxiing. Any traffic-jam at the end of the runway is a catastrophe, and yet, since on operations of this sort every drop of fuel is needed, planes set course as soon as the undercart is up. Therefore everyone has to start up engines simultaneously and not dawdle over taxiing.

To complicate matters, at Sumburgh the runway was very short and ended up at the foot of a hill. What you had to do was to tear the plane off the ground at 3000 revs, 16 boost and 15 degrees of flap, and climb before you reached the safe flying speed of 180 m.p.h..

As expected, the last three Mosquitoes, with their radiators at 130° C. and white smoke coming out of their exhausts, could not catch up. The infuriated pilots had to pack in altogether to avoid dangerous internal leakages of glycol.

11.25—Sixteen Mosquitoes, led by Max Guedj, set course 069 degrees over the North Sea.

12.30—It was pouring with rain and, like a ghostly school of porpoises, the planes kept close together just above the long swell. Snow and spray bespattered the windshields, and the crews, peering forward into the murk, were having a grim time.

Economical cruising speed—220 m.p.h.—1800 revs and 0 boost. The navigators kept fiddling about with the fuel-cocks and glancing at the gauges. From time to time the sea and the mist merged into an opaque moving wall through which the aircraft plunged anxiously.

When that happened Max switched on his downward recognition light and the light skipped from wave to wave piercing the damp white wisps of vapour. The planes edged still closer together.

The Mosquitoes carved their way through the murk. Where the formation had passed, there remained, long after the sound of engines had died away, straight swathes cut through the moisture-laden air by the burning exhaust gases.

12.40—The Mustangs seemed to have missed the rendezvous in this thick weather. Max made the two squadrons do a wide and highly dangerous 360-degree turn. The pilots concentrated for dear life—getting into another bloke's slipstream, ten feet above the icy water, would be certain death.

Max's manoeuvre would give the Mustangs an extra two minutes at this game of blind-man's buff. Not that he was banking too much on it. With horizontal visibility reduced to a few dozen feet, two formations could pass very close to one another without being aware of it. You couldn't ask the impossible of those fighter-pilots, alone in their cockpit and with no navigator. How could they arrive at a given second at the intersection in space of two arbitrary co-ordinates which left no mark on the featureless surface of the sea?

Help from R/T was out of the question. The German goniometers and listening-posts were on the *qui vive*.

Max gave it up and set course again on the target.

The observer, his face glued to the perspex, tried to penetrate the fog. The treacherous Norwegian coast must be near, with its mountains falling sheer into the sea. How many Coastal Command planes had blindly crashed into the granite cliffs of the Skajaergaard! Max's pilots knew all about it and, hands contracted on the throttle levers, they were ready to fling their planes into a left turn in a fraction of a second.

12.47—Max suddenly broke the R/T silence. It was the first words that the Y service W.A.A.F.s at Wick and Kirkwall entered on the blank sheet before them headed 'Radio telephony. Communications. Op. 005718.'

He shouted into the microphone: 'Revolver leader calling. Look out for ship ahead 11 o'clock. Shark Blue, sink it before it uses radio.'

The ship, whatever it was, would obviously radio the size and course of the Mosquito formation to the German defensive network. No time to waste. Now was an opportunity for Max's superb training of his crews to show itself.

Automatically Shark Blue 1, without having seen the ship, but knowing where it must be relative to his leader, reduced throttle, changed to fine pitch and turned right. There, between two veils of rain, was a large trawler, sparks twittering on its aerial. None too soon!

The observer had already switched on the sight and now he fired two rockets from under each wing.

Woooooofffoooff . . . the four missiles glided along the rails and swooped towards the hazy outline bobbing up and down.

Left of the bridge, near the stumpy mast, there seemed to be a light winking—Morse probably. F/Lt. MacGregor, Shark Blue 1, felt a slight jar under his feet.

A terrific flash of orange flame, reflected by the waves . . . debris . . . jets of steam . . . It was all over—the trawler, sliced in two, was. swallowed up.

Shark Blue 1 turned tight left at full throttle to catch up the formation, and his No. 2, still dazzled by the explosion, did his best to follow.

MacGregor shook his observer, who seemed to be falling asleep, and shouted to him to buck up. He got a spurt of blood full in the face. That winking light had been a machine-gun, and the jar had been a stupid little 7.7 bullet. But that single bullet had pierced the hydraulic fluid tank and had then ricochetted. The observer had got it smack in the chest.

The dangerous choking fumes from the Girling fluid were already filling the cabin, and the pilot quickly put on his mask and switched the oxygen full on.

About turn and back to Scotland, to save the observer, if possible. The Mosquito disappeared, heading west.[12]

12.53—There was the rock wall, with the sea breaking on it and enormous masses of spray disappearing into the fog.

'Revolver turning port, steering zero one five.'

Was it an island or the mainland? All those cliffs looked much

---

[12] F/Lt. MacGregor, stupefied by the fumes, ditched his plane and was picked up off Scapa Flow the next morning by a destroyer. But the North Sea in January is unforgiving and he died in Kirkwall hospital two days later.

the same, and there seemed to be nothing particular to distinguish this one.

'Stadstsland Point,' said Langley in a matter-of-fact tone of voice. During the two years he had been operating in these parts he had memorised every detail of the coast.

Course 015 degrees, towards the north and the dangers of the Arctic Circle. The rain was now mixed with snow, which calmed the phosphorescent waves a little.

Having started in the dubious daylight of our winter, the planes were now gradually being swallowed up by the indeterminate shadows of the polar night. Only one hour left of this pale light in which nothing showed up sharp. They must attack quickly.

The fog now lifted and gave place to thick snow, flying horizontally and describing a whirling spiral round the propellers. The observers were hard at work switching on carburettor heaters, the de-icing gear, fluid pumps for the propellers, pitot-head and gyro-intake heaters.

Ping—crack—crack—ping—the bits of ice detached from the propellers bounced off the wooden fuselage, which reverberated like a drum.

'Bloody weather.'

Max did not reply, he was thinking out the plan of campaign. Shark would hug the left flank of the fjord, Revolver the right, and the two Blue sections would take the centre. After that, everybody—at least everybody who got through the concentrated flak—would reform round the lighthouse on Barroy Island.

'Target ahead in ten minutes, skipper.'

'Thanks.'

Over there, where the horizon was clear, there was a pink streak, the only touch of colour in the grey and white landscape—grey aircraft with white bellies, grey sea, white cliffs, grey clouds. It was the sun on the desolate ice-pack off North Cape.

Max remembered—July 1942. He was flying a Beaufighter. For hours his mates and he had been flying over the monotonous jumble of ice-floes searching for the Murmansk convoy, dispersed by the *Tirpitz* and the Junkers 88s. Twenty-two merchant ships out of twenty-eight, most of them American, had been sunk. The smoking remains were being crushed by the ice, on which the survivors were left wandering about.

'Revolver and Shark aircraft, open up. Target ahead in three minutes. Shark keep to the left, Revolver to the right, Blue Sections up the middle. Turning-in point and rendezvous after attack Barroy Light. Good luck.'

There was Vest Fjord. Careful now—3000 revs, plus 16 boost, propellers at fine pitch, cannon and rockets armed. Barroy Island, with its black-and-white striped lighthouse, semaphore and radar station. An 88 battery too, apparently. Three ochre balls suddenly appeared just below the clouds, about 700 feet above the aircraft, like three blotches of ink on a blotting-pad— probably a sighting shot. The sirens at Elvegaard and Narvik must be going full blast.

'Revolver and Shark, attack.'

The main fjord now, flanked by cliffs 1500 feet high surmounted by glaciers.

No flak yet? A miracle.

The formation swept into the fjord at 375 m.p.h., Shark and Revolver hugging the hillsides, and in the middle, like a rake sweeping over the open channel, the six Mosquitoes of the Blue sections line-abreast. At the foot of a Cyclopean pile of rocks embedded in the snow the Revolver planes passed the charred remains of a German destroyer which had met its end there on 13th April 1940.

Suddenly the main fjord widened and split up into four fingers, Hergang, Narvik, Romback and Elvegaard Fjords. Narvik was straight ahead, with its black roofs, wooden church steeple and piles of timber on the wharves. A few fishing-boats, an old beached paddle-steamer.

Max methodically cast his mind back to the Intelligence photos. The target was in Romback Fjord, a sinuous corridor three-quarters of a mile wide, with walls half a mile high. At this moment it was roofed in by a thick cloud, and right at the end, moored hard against the vertical wall of rock, must be the tanker.

'Look out, flak!'

The Sharks had veered to the right towards the opening of the fjord. Max passed over the town like a whirlwind, banking vertically. The sky filled with flashes and tracer bullets.

The six Blue Mosquitoes hurled themselves against the big destroyer which was blazing away with all its guns. It disappeared at once in the trails and explosions of forty-eight rockets which ripped open its hull like tissue-paper.

A bright light filled the sky, there was a graceful parabola of black smoke, and a Mosquito crashed. A second disappeared in fragments among the pine trees on a mountainside. A parachute broke loose from a third, whose wing had been torn off by a direct hit from an 88 shell.

A web of light was being spread across the valley by at least twenty flak emplacements concealed among the rocks. The puffs from the 20-mm. spread a white carpet round the planes zigzagging madly between the strings of tracer.

The two Sperrbrechers and the escort vessels were moored in staggered formation and blocked the entrance to the fjord. The planes would have to run the gauntlet of their cross-fire. Between them they had sixty 20-mm. guns and twenty-two 37-mm., which could put up a wall of 500 shells a second.

One Mosquito, probably hit among its cargo of rockets, exploded ten yards above an escort vessel and covered it with a sheet of burning petrol. The ammunition on the ship's deck immediately went off, mowing down the flak crews. The aircraft behind, aiming blindly into the blaze, let go its rockets, which pulverised the ship.

The hellish noise re-echoed from the valley walls. The flak and the roar of the engines started up avalanches which swept down the mountainsides into the sea with a rumbling roar, as if nature herself were in revolt against this man-made din.

But a new sound now intervened, the irregular metallic drone of B.M.W. engines. Twenty Focke-Wulfs emerged over Bjervick. From Bardufoss airfield they had sneaked under the clouds into the valley and now hurled themselves at 400 m.p.h. on. the trapped Mosquitoes.

Max was still in the lead. Tilting his Mosquito from side to side, he had managed to get across the barrage from the flak ships unscathed.

Right at the top of the fjord, merging into the mountain, was the tanker, camouflaged with irregular black and white stripes. Low in the water, funnel well aft, it was embedded in the ice. Max had its silhouette clear in his sights.

The recoil of his four cannon firing was like a mule kicking under his feet. He waited so as to fire his rockets at point-blank range. In the meantime, to neutralise the flak, he went on firing his cannon, and his 20-mm. shells went whining over the ice, exploding in succession over the ship's hull.

'Rockets on—the whole lot!'

Langley, the observer, tense in his seat—a mere spectator, at the mercy of his pilot's skill—armed the complete salvo of eight rockets, the equivalent of a broadside from a 10,000-ton cruiser. Max leant forward and his eyes tightened. His finger touched the firing button.

At the exact moment that he was going to fire, his Mosquito was suddenly catapulted sideways by a terrific explosion. Instinctively, in spite of the fearful pain which twisted his guts, Max pulled with all his might on the stick. The hull, the masts, the rocks, the trees—everything whirled before his eyes. The plane shot viciously upwards and disappeared into the clouds.

Max straightened out the skidding plane and, over Langley's collapsed body, saw that the starboard engine was belching flame through its shattered cowling. He now had the horrid job of flying through the cloud surrounded by mountains, with all his instruments haywire, to say nothing of the searing pain of his wound.

The plane vibrated dangerously. Steady now—feather starboard propeller—fire extinguishers. Still that terrible pain and the warm blood trickling down his legs inside his trousers.

Suddenly, blue sky above the smooth white cloud-layer. His observer was dead, his blood spattered all over the cabin, the instrument panel, the controls, the windows. His gyros and artificial horizon, toppled by the shock, were now settling down again.

Above all, he mustn't faint. He turned 180 degrees left. The fire was out, dirty foam oozed through the. cracked cowling. What was happening down below? An occasional string of flak came up through the clouds, the black bursts looking quite incongruous in that absurd calm.

The rockets were still on their rails. What a temptation, just to call it a day . . . fly home over the clouds . . . quite peacefully, all the way to Scotland . . . wait for the radio-compass to show land below . . . bale out. After all, he had brought back a Beau on one engine all the way from the Bay of Biscay, and a Mosquito was much easier. Yes, but that time the mission was completed. What were his planes doing? What about the tanker? He could hear nothing on the R/T, but the transmitter still seemed to be working. He had made up his mind.

'Revolver leader here. I am going to do another run.'

A glance at the chromo. The sea must be below by now. Cautious descent through the cloud, keeping his plane as level as possible; a few wisps of thicker vapour and there was the grey, heaving water.

He turned, getting his bearings. There was Barroy Island again. He pushed his unharmed port engine to 'emergency', wound the rudder trimmer right over to relieve his left foot, which was getting tired through having to push hard on the rudder-bar all the time.

There was Narvik. Whatever happened, he mustn't faint. The pain made everything exceptionally clear and lucid—Focke-Wulfs buzzing and zooming up and down the fjord like wasps on a window-pane, Mosquitoes in flames shedding fragments of wing and fuselage on the snow, pillars of black smoke drifting over the water. Was that all that was left of his planes?

In that small inlet, an iridescent patch of oil bestrewn with the remains of a ship; a few men in yellow Mae Wests, swimming; enormous bubbles bursting on the surface; further on, a beached destroyer, its side gaping.

The flak was still there, as savage as a tornado, an impassable barrier. The Mosquito, pursued by four Focke-Wulfs, their cannon lit up with flashes, skimmed the sea. He was so low that the slipstream from his propeller created a wake behind him, shivering on the black water dotted with spurts of foam from the shells.

He must keep going at all costs.

A Focke-Wulf was twenty yards behind the Mosquito, weaving to deliver the *coup de grâce.* It fired at point-blank range. The shells ripped through the fuselage and hammered into the armour plating protecting Max's back. One thousand yards still to go. Five hundred. The other engine was now on fire, the flames gnawing at the wooden main-spar. A piece of shrapnel had smashed his sight—now he would have to fire his rockets at fifty yards range in order not to miss.

The Mosquito oscillated in its flight, like a runner lurching, and another Focke-Wulf now fired into it, its shells bursting on the tanker as well as on the Mosquito.

There was a flash of flame as the eight rockets sped on their errand.

The thunder of the explosion reverberating in the fjord was so terrific that the inhabitants of Narvik rushed panic-stricken into the streets, thinking that the mountain was coming down.

Later the Norwegians found a winch from the ship 2000 yards from the explosion.

The Mosquito disappeared in the sea of flame which swallowed up all the trees on the slopes for several hundred yards.

It was snowing again, and the flakes were black with soot. Four Mosquitoes, four crews, utterly exhausted, battled through the black starless Arctic night to get back to their base. Four Mosquitoes out of nineteen.

***

And that is the story of Max Guedj. He was another of those 'emigrant mercenaries' of the Free French Air Force, just like Mouchotte, Maridor, Labouchère, Fayolle, Pijeaud and Schloesig. French history is rich in acts of heroism, but there are not so many that are quite of this quality.

May Frenchmen bow their heads when they hear his name.

May they remember that Englishmen in the R.A.F often paid him this tribute. It is the least that the greatest hero of the French Air Force from 1939 to 1945 deserves.

Hector Bolitho, the popular writer and playwright, mobilised during the war by the historical section of the Services, has a striking portrait of Max Guedj in his book *Task for Coastal Command* (pp. 123-4):

'A French pilot serving with the R.A.F., who has made many audacious attacks on shipping along the coasts of his country, led fifteen Mosquitoes which crippled two minesweepers yesterday afternoon . . .

'Getting a story out of this French pilot is like opening oysters with your bare hands. But I also am arrogant, and I won't leave this diary without some mention of his work. When he becomes old and charitable and in need of gentleness, he may show this page to his grandchildren, as a bait for their respect. Ever since "D" day he has led attacks, closer and closer into the harbours and rivers of the Bay [of Biscay], ruthlessly, with a sort of cold intellectual persistence. The impersonal patriotism that compels an educated Frenchman to fight like this reveals the will that must be at the heart of that country, behind the vacillation of politicians and the sophisticated cynicism of Paris.

'I once tried to make him talk, but he looked at me with eyes that said, "I am wholly certain of myself. My mind is as cold and sharp as a new razor blade and I won't tell you anything. I am being polite to you because I am a gentleman, but I wish you to know that I long ago learned to rule my heart with my mind so it is no use trying to appeal to me with any of your writer's tricks."

'I filled in the ten minutes of the interview with nervous small talk, all the time aware that I was defeated. And that he knew it.

'His dark eyes, "like polished damsons," brook no interference with his authority, and he has the rare blessing of believing that he is always right. He is what is described in wartime as "a born leader". It is revealed in his walk and his voice. What this talent will achieve in peace-time is a theme which fascinates me. War finds room for all these Caesars whose moral courage is frightening. I would like to meet this French pilot in ten years' time and see whither his fierce will has led him.'

The periodical *Flight*, in its number of 1st February 1945, has a page dedicated to the six great 'aces' of Coastal Command. Round the Coastal Command crest are the portraits of: Wing-Commander G. D. Six, D.S.O., D.F.C. and Bar; Group Captain the Hon. Max Aitken, D.S.O., D.F.C. and Bar; Wing-Commander Atkinson, D.S.O., D.F.C.; the Australian Wing-Commander McDonnell, D.S.O., D.F.C.; S/Ldr. Pritchard, D.F.C.; and finally S/Ldr. 'Maurice', D.S.O., D.F.C. and Bar.

NOTE ON THE MOSQUITO

In 1938 the De Havilland company decided to construct, at its own expense and without an official order—in fact against the advice of the R.A.F. experts—an exceptionally fast, unarmed bomber. It was the same theory as Ernst Udet's, and the Luftwaffe paid heavily for its mistake in the first two years of the war.

De Havilland, however, succeeded where all other designers failed. The Mosquito did fly higher and faster than most of the fighters that were put up against it.

The Mosquito was a masterpiece, and revolutionary from the tip of its rudder to the end of its ailerons. It was built of laths of birch and balsawood ply glued under pressure, and its wings and fuselage were covered with doped cloth. Two Rolls-Royce 'Merlin' engines propelled the prototype at over 375 m.p.h. The crew of two, pilot and observer, sat side by side, as in the front seat of a car, and enjoyed perfect forward vision.

As soon as the drawings, the calculations and the wind-tunnel tests were finished, the Air Ministry gave in—the evidence was conclusive, and Geoffrey de Havilland and C. C. Walker had hit the jackpot.

'An ugly plane is sometimes all right, but a graceful-looking plane always flies beautifully.' John, Geoffrey's brother, who killed himself in 1943 testing a Mosquito, told me that one day at Hatfield. The Mosquito's lines were certainly breath-takingly clean and graceful. Only the Messerschmitt 262 could be compared with it, but the Messerschmitt was more aggressive, coarser, more vicious-looking—more Germanic, in a word.

I saw my first Mosquito at Cranwell. It was the prototype Mark 1, W 4050. Caught by the bad weather, it had to make an acrobatic landing on our field. Pale grey on top and sky-blue beneath, it slid between the sheets of rain falling from the leaden sky like a trout effortlessly making its way up its home stream. The U/T pilots training at Cranwell were all on the grass outside the Watch-office in the pelting rain and watched fascinated. That same evening three of them asked for a transfer to twin-engined aircraft.

The Mosquito was such a superb design that, before it had flown, the R.A.F. ordered a Photo-Recce version and a day-and night-fighter version. The bomber model first flew on 25th November 1940, the fighter on 15th May 1941 and the reconnaissance plane on 10th June 1941. On 20th September 1941 the prototype successfully carried out a difficult photo-trip in daylight—Brest—La Pallice—Bordeaux, with return via Paris. Geoffrey de Havilland flew it himself; he was chased by three Messerschmitt 109s, but easily out-distanced them at 23,000 feet.

The fighter version was fantastically manoeuvrable. With one engine stopped and the propeller feathered, four cannon and four machine-guns in the nose and 500 gallons in the tanks the Mosquito F. Mk. 2 could easily do a slow roll immediately after take-off.

Two years later over a thousand Mosquitoes of various types were in service with the R.A.F. Four squadrons bombed Berlin every day, day and night, each plane carrying a two-ton bomb. In 320 raids they lost only twelve planes. In spite of all their efforts the Germans never managed to catch these Mosquitoes, which kept Berlin in a state of perpetual alert. And the damage to the enemy capital was not only psychological. It is enough to recall that a Mosquito with a crew of two, and two engines, carried into the heart of Germany half a ton more bomb-load than the Flying Fortress, and 50 m.p.h. faster.

It was perhaps on low-level daylight raids that Mosquitoes brought off their most sensational feats, in particular the destruction of the Gestapo H.Q.s at Oslo and at Copenhagen, and also the famous Amiens prison show. In the course of these the planes flying at roof-top level placed their bombs slap through the windows of the target.

When the Mosquito fighters in 1942-43 began their 'ranger' flights, they terrorised the Luftwaffe in its remotest bases. Hurtling along in pairs at 375 m.p.h., they ambushed German planes deep inside their own territory. This individualistic way of fighting was the most exciting method of air warfare, rather like the hit-and-run tactics of the corsairs of old.

Drake himself would have been proud of this operational report, signed by S/Ldr. Scherf, D.S.O., an Australian, on 23rd September 1943:

'We took off at 1415 hours, in two Mosquitoes, S/Ldr. Cleveland being the other pilot. We set course for North Germany across the Baltic.

'Over the sea I saw a plane. It was a Dornier. He had seen us and the black trails from his exhausts showed that he was flying with maximum boost. However, I caught up with him quite easily and shot him down into the sea with one burst from my four cannon.

'We crossed the German coast at Kubitzer north of Rostock and we soon afterwards met two Junker 87s. I turned after one, while Cleveland went after the other. My first two bursts, 60 degrees correction, missed because he was turning very tight, but the third was on the mark and the Stuka went over on its back, burst into flames and crashed.

'As we flew along the coast a little further south we saw an airfield and several planes in the circuit. A Heinkel 177 was just making its approach. I didn't want to cross the airfield, because of the flak, so I attacked him head-on, from below. The enemy plane crashed into the bay in flames. Time, 1552 hours.

'As I turned I saw Cleveland chasing a twin-engined Junkers 88. His shells were ripping bits out of the enemy, who was beginning to smoke. I did not see how it ended because at that moment I spotted two Dornier 18s moored in a creek. I dived on them. The first exploded and sank, but the second weathered three bursts, to my regret.

'The flak started up just then and I broke, hugging the dunes. I found myself underneath two Junkers 88s flying in formation. The first broke up in the air, but as I was attacking the second I was hit by a shell from a 20-mm. automatic battery which tore off one of my drop-tanks and damaged my rudder. After retrimming my plane, I set off at full throttle after the second Junker 88 and shot him down. While all this was going on I lost sight of Cleveland and set course for home by myself.

'After twenty minutes' flying over the sea I saw Cleveland and caught up with him. He was flying with difficulty, on one engine, which was constantly missing. Over the R/T he told me he had brought down two planes and destroyed a third on the ground. He asked me to write to his wife Jeanie and warn her he couldn't get back to England. Rather than be made prisoner he was going to have a shot at making it to Sweden. I said goodbye to Cleveland and wished him luck.

'I then passed a German naval convoy and used up the rest of my ammunition on a minesweeper. There was a lot of flak and my observer got hit in the right side.

'Just north of Heligoland I had the sun in my eyes and ran slap into a flight of seagulls. Twenty-seven of them fouled my aircraft and caused considerable damage—aerial torn off, port engine stopped, port aileron jammed, every forward pane of perspex broken, and we were covered with blood and feathers.

'We landed at our home station at 1845 hours. I asked for confirmation of five planes shot down and one destroyed on the ground, and, on behalf of S/Ldr. Cleveland, D.F.C., two shot down and one destroyed on the ground.'

Not a bad day's work!

At the beginning of 1944 Coastal Command began to replace Beaufighters with Mosquitoes on some of its units. Most of these Mosquitoes were equipped with two sets of four rockets each, weighing 60 lb. apiece, and four 20-mm. cannon. The eight rockets had the same power on impact as eight 6-in. shells. The Mosquitoes under Max Guedj's orders were equipped in this way.

On other Mosquitoes they kept four machine-guns and, instead of the four 20-mm. cannon, they installed a 6-pounder

(57-mm.) anti-tank gun in the nose and slung two more large tanks under the wings, which doubled their radius of action.

One of these Mosquitoes had what can only be described as an artillery duel with a German destroyer off the Spanish coast. Keeping 2000 yards away from the ship, i.e. out of range of the 20-mm. automatic flak, the Mosquito fired fifty armour-piercing shells, of which thirty-eight scored hits. With its hull, furnaces and turbines all bored through, the destroyer had to heave-to, a defenceless target. The next morning two Polish Coastal Command Liberators were whistled up and sank it with bombs.

The Mosquito XVI had a wing-span of 54 feet 2 inches, a length of 44 feet 6 inches and a wing area of 420 square feet. Its laden weight was about 11 tons and it was powered by two Rolls-Royce 'Merlin' engines of 1600 h.p. each, giving it a maximum speed of 435 m.p.h. at 25,000 feet. Its ceiling was 36,000 feet, fully laden, and its range nearly 2500 miles. Pretty sensational figures!

Four Mosquitoes were transformed into civil aircraft in 1943, with three bunks in the bomb-bay. These planes, flying for British Overseas Airways Corporation, carried out a regular London-Stockholm service, carrying diplomatic mail and V.I.P.s over occupied Europe. These planes were naturally unarmed.

Only one of these Mosquitoes was ever intercepted, and that was in February 1944. It was cornered over Denmark by several Messerschmitt 163 rocket planes. The pilot knew that his opponents had fuel for only a few dozen seconds, and that if he wasn't brought down within two minutes he was O.K. So he hurled his plane about madly and his passengers, emerging from their slumbers with a start and numb with cold, found themselves bouncing about inside the fuselage like ping-pong balls. The pilot finally got away by diving vertically for the sea at such a speed that the plane nearly broke up. Two of the passengers had burst eardrums, and the third—a British diplomat friend of mine—swore to high heaven that nothing would ever induce him to step inside a plane again. He has kept his word, but all the same he, like so many others, owed his life to the Mosquito.

CHAPTER EIGHT

THE TWILIGHT OF THE GODS

On the vast deserted airfield at Langenhagen a pall of soot was falling from the fires in Hanover. Nothing remained of the hangars but twisted steel skeletons. The bomb craters were in serried rows like cells in a beehive. The long runway for the jet planes was a mass of shattered blocks of concrete. It was an apocalyptic landscape of ruin and desolation.

The dispersal tracks ran off into the woods, but they weren't much use, as the very trees were in flames. From time to time came a crash as the tanks of a Junkers 88 or a Focke-Wulf 190 exploded, revealing the uselessness of camouflage in such an avalanche of steel and flame.

On land, at sea and in the air the jaws of the trap were relentlessly tightening. The solid phalanxes of Fortresses kept on passing overhead. The Sherman tanks and the tank-destroyers rumbled eastwards over the dislocated slabs of the Osnabrück Autobahn. Letting loose their murderous salvoes of rockets and hollow-charge shells, the Typhoons harried the last S.P. guns and the last Panthers from hedge to hedge.

The Lancasters with their ten-ton 'Grand Slams' were crushing the last U-boats deep inside their concrete pens at Bremen and in the Baltic. The Tempests and Mustangs, roaming the

German air at roof-top level, picked off the last 'Long-Nose' Focke-Wulfs and Messerschmitts.

For the Luftwaffe, April 1945 was a bloody twilight. . .

A Spitfire XIV from the Canadian Tactical Reconnaissance Wing dived down out of the top layer of cumulus and began to describe a wide circle round Langenhagen. The pilot carefully lined up the ruins of the airfield against the graduated marks on his wings and began to take his obliques . . . 40 degrees . . . 45 degrees . . . 70 degrees . . . 90 degrees . . . click . . . click . . . click.

The film in the camera wound round and the hand of the counter on the instrument panel clicked round. Five more . . . three more. Waste of time, thought the pilot, the airfield was dead. One left.

Finished now. Suddenly the pilot instinctively tightened his plane's diving turn—a Volkswagen, zigzagging between the bomb craters, had appeared between the ruins of two hangars. A second's hesitation. The Spitfire was at a height of 1000 feet and was about to attack, when the flak started up. First only one clip of five shells, then it started coming up from everywhere.

Climbing full-throttle for the clouds, the Canadian noticed, stuck on a wooden tower surrounded by burning trees, an automatic four-barrelled 20-mm. firing through the smoke.

Much too accurate, that Jerry flak! Why risk your neck for one car lost in that wilderness!

Back at Twente, the Wing's base, the pilot made his report: 'Not a plane left on the ground. All the airfield installations completely wiped out. I took my photos only as a matter of form. Still some flak, though, I don't know why.'

It was just after 5 p.m. Langenhagen had been under threat of attack or under actual attack since dawn, but things were calming down. The Spitfire had just disappeared into the clouds and the flak had stopped firing. The gun-crews surrounded by the fires caused by the last raid hastened to get their guns and ammunition out of harm's reach. The Volkswagen started up again and emerged from behind the remains of a wall, followed by another car and a lorry.

From among the ruins swarms of men and women appeared, carrying baskets full of earth, and spades. S.S. men were urging them on, machine-pistols at the ready. All these miserable wretches, their wasted frames covered by the striped rags of the deported, started filling in the craters on the main runway.

At the four corners of the airfield there was a series of grassy mounds; in front of each was a carefully camouflaged cement apron. Each was an underground hangar. Two had collapsed inwards, four were hopelessly blocked by the bombing, but six were intact.

The heavy steel doors moved aside smoothly on their well-greased runners—all except one, twisted out of true by the blast of a large bomb; this had to be forced open.

In front of each shelter the cars deposited four men and one box marked: 'Deutsche Waffen und Fabriken—5 mm. 5 R4M—50.'

Somewhere a generator must have started up, for the bulbs let into the walls of the casemates came on and lit up the thoroughbred outlines of Messerschmitt 262 jet fighters.

While the fitters got ready the system of pulleys and cables which hauled the planes up the ramp to the apron, the pilots made their preparations in silence. One of them was a Major-General, though still quite a young man. Over their Luftwaffe uniforms they drew on flying-suits made of pliable black leather.

Two miles away, on a hill in the depths of Osterwald forest, stood a shooting-box, covered with camouflage netting and branches. From its window Langenhagen Airfield could be seen.

It was the control centre of Lehr Geschwader No. 1. There were the usual Flugmeldedienst personnel round the telephone and the maps—officers and N.C.Os. In a corner, unexpected in such surroundings, stood three civilians, a woman and two men. On the wall was a loud-speaker.

Everyone in that room, with its walls of rough-hewn pine and its strong smell of resin, instinctively looked away from the loud-speaker as a message came crackling out of it:

'Achtung, Achtung. 140 Flying Fortresses reported by Borkum radar, course 095, height 23,000 feet. Fighter escort. General anti-aircraft alert in areas Bremen, Hamburg, Kiel, Lübeck. . . .'

The three civilians exchanged glances. For four years they had been working to perfect the most terrible of all aerial weapons, and fate had decreed that the first test should also be the last, the Luftwaffe's final throw.

Professor Willy Messerschmitt had built the Messerschmitt 262 jet 'Kampfzerstoerer,' 600 m.p.h., faster than the fastest Allied fighter. Professor Fuchs had perfected the Ez 42 automatic sight, with which the pilot was mathematically certain to hit the target. Fraulein Doktor E. Schwartz, from the D.M.W. laboratories at Lübeck, was the inventor of the R4M rocket, whose ballistic properties and 1-lb explosive charge were sufficient to pulverise the largest Allied bomber at 900 yards' range.

Everything was now ready. From Langenhagen six of the twelve Messerschmitt 262s sent direct from the Oberammergau experimental works—some had not even received one coat of paint—were about to hurl themselves into the fray, the first to be equipped with the Ez 42 and R4Ms. They were to be flown by General der Flieger Gordon Gollob, Commander of the Iron Cross with Swords, Oak Leaves and Diamonds, and five selected pilots.

In the first of the underground hangars a phone had rung, giving the order to start. A sergeant had hastily jotted down the information on the American raid, and rushed over with the sheet of paper to where Gollob sat under his plane's wing.

Two hundred yards beyond, Oberleutnant Flans already sat in his cockpit and kept an eye on his chief. He felt uncomfortable in his special strapped parachute whose flat duralumin spare oxygen-bottle dug painfully into his thigh. But it was too late to change its position.

When Hans saw Gollob glance at the paper and then jump into his plane, his fears vanished. For the first time since early on the previous day he relaxed. He had been shot down just as he was about to land on his home base at Lechfeld, and dragged out of the remains of his plane, miraculously unhurt. He had just sunk into a heavy sleep disturbed by the nightmares caused by delayed shock when his Colonel hauled him out of bed at midnight. The General wanted him at once. That was how he learnt that he had had the honour of being selected for a special mission.

He had sped in a car through the rest of the night, arriving at Langenhagen just as a Fortress raid was in progress. In a shelter, shaken by the bomb explosions and choked with dust, he had been told by the General what was expected of him. All day long he and his comrades had waited, to the nerve-shattering accompaniment of walls crashing, guns firing and bombs whistling down.

He was hungry—since yesterday's dinner he had only had one slice of black bread and a sausage—and also very thirsty. Not a drop of water in the place, the underground pipes had all been smashed.

Now, blessed relief, they were off. The fitters were busy round his plane. The two-stroke Riedel auxiliary starter-motor was in place and a fitter pushed a metal rod into the air-intake and then gave it a sharp pull. The irregular firing warned Hans that the tricky moment was at hand. When the engine reached 4000 revs he slowly engaged the heavy motor. The concave blades of the turbine began to spin with a crescendo of noise like a siren. He opened the fuel cocks and the cockpit filled with the sickly stench of paraffin vapour. The starter magneto crackled and the screaming of the turbine gave place to a deeper throbbing roar.

Hans breathed a sigh of relief. There had been no back-fire. Under his tailplane stretched a long band of grass and earth charred by the burning breath of the Jumo 004B jet unit.

Hans methodically repeated the process for the other turbine.

The fuel intake pressures began to settle down. He made sure his two power-units were perfectly synchronised and then looked across to see how the others were doing. They too seemed to have started up safely at the first attempt. They never gave you properly tuned and serviced planes like this on squadron, thought Hans bitterly. At Lechfeld it was rare for two out of four Messerschmitt 262s to take off without mishap.

Gollob's plane began to move. Taking-off was going to be even stickier than usual. For a start, there was no question of tractors towing them to the end of the runway, and they would therefore have to taxi over half a mile under their own power along the bomb-damaged dispersal track—hoping they wouldn't get caught and strafed by Allied fighters!

Hans's fitters kept his plane running straight, while he carefully stayed below the 5000 revs allowed for taxiing. The procession moved up between the rows of smoking fir-trees, stopping from time to time to allow the fitters to clear the track of branches; the smell of burning wood and hot paraffin reached his nostrils.

The temperature was going up—450 degrees at the intake and 550 degrees at the compressor. He must not overheat, otherwise when he took off at full throttle he might easily burn out the rotor blades. And he would need every ounce of power to get his heavily laden plane off the ground.

'Schnell, Jaguar, schnell!'

It was Gollob, telling them to get a move on.

At last the whole Schwarm was lined up at the end of the runway. Hans was too busy making sure his seat was the right height and the hood properly shut to see the first two pairs take off.

Now it was his turn. The fitters helped him line up his plane. Brakes still on, he revved up to 8000. Then, the temperature already at 600 degrees, he let her go. The machine began to gather speed, while the strident whistle which had been drilling his eardrums began to abate.

60 . . . 100 . . . 150 . . . 175 m.p.h. He had already covered a whole mile of runway and he still couldn't get her off the ground. Every time a wheel went over a recently filled-in crater Hans felt the whole aircraft vibrate terribly.

For one moment he had the impression that the plane just could not take off with the weight of those forty-eight rockets plus their rails under the wing.

The end of the runway rushed up at appalling speed. The clock showed nearly 185 m.p.h., but every time he gingerly eased the stick back the plane's nose would, just lift slightly and then fall back on the front wheel of the tricycle undercart with a heavy thud.

Desperately he pushed the lever regulating the angle of in-cidence of the tailplane and the bumps stopped at once. He was in the air now and he wrestled with the stick to keep his plane on an even keel over the treetops. Keeping his eyes fixed on the four aircraft ahead of him, he raised his undercart and his flaps. His speed increased at once—350 . . . 400 . . . 450 m.p.h. . . . and he began to climb.

They were now at 33,000 feet and, in spite of the numbing cold, Hans could feel his underclothes sticky with sweat.

In parallel combat formation—flight-leaders 200 yards

apart—the six jets, guided by the Bremen controller, were closing with the American bombers at the rate of 500 m.p.h. At that speed they could take it easy—no danger of being intercepted or caught napping. Hans turned and admired the aircraft; even those with the thick ochre and green camouflage on a grey background retained the purity of their lines—the thin, swept wings with their underslung turbo-jet units, the pear-shaped fuselage with its high tailplane, like the perfectly balanced lines of a shark's body.

'Noch schneller, Jaguar!'[13]

The twelve white trails from the turbines now showed a trace of black smoke. The horizon-line was slightly higher up the windshield nose in the perspex and the A.S.I. steadied at 550 m.p.h. Hans began to feel the controls vibrate under his hand. He checked up on his blind-flying instruments—you never knew what might happen at these very high speeds.

'Jaguar! Caruso 240—alle nach links!'[14] The Schwarmfuehrer's voice in the phones nearly burst his ear-drums. He started his left turn at once, while Gollob and his Katschmark turned under him. The formation of Flying Fortresses which Hans now saw was not the big square composed of rows of bright dots that it seems from the ground. It was an enormous block of planes, spaced out in the sky in layers as far as the eye could reach, and gently moving up and down and from left to right among the dark 88-mm. flak bursts. The fighters of the escort were dancing about on the fringe.

---

[13] 'Faster, Jaguar!'
[14] 'Jaguar! Caruso 240—everyone turn left.'

Hans switched on his Ez 42, and in the reflector the gyroscope began to dance and hum. He then inserted a cartridge into the seat-ejector mechanism—just in case.

Leaning forward, his left thumb on the arming switch for the rockets, his right forefinger on the firing-button for the cannon, he watched to see how Gollob went into action.

The Messerschmitt 262 was not so fast that the classic technique—frontal attack followed by half-roll, and then break by diving—was out of the question. The 262s skimmed over the formation, corkscrewing through the echelons of impotent fighters. They then attacked the lower portion of the second box of sixty-four Fortresses.

Hans, who was having trouble keeping up with his leader, passed a squadron of P-51 Mustangs, who quickly scattered and jettisoned their drop-tanks, but he had no time to fire at them. He half lost control of his plane as he turned with a lot of skid, and when he righted himself he found he was in the thick of the Fortresses.

The big four-engined aircraft were wreathed in the smoke of their innumerable heavy machine-guns and seemed to be dancing in his windshield and rushing towards him. He was in a tunnel of bombers and tracer bullets.

He aimed at one haphazardly as he flew, and fired his four cannon and a salvo of twenty rockets all at the same time. Like incandescent arrows the rockets slipped smoothly along their runners and caught up the cannon shells converging on the B-17s tailplane.

The next thing he knew he was flying in a cloud of aluminium debris. A severed wing with its two engines still turning was spinning down in flames, a body was falling dangling on an unopened parachute, and a ripped-open fuselage was vomiting thick white smoke. Bang in front of him under two oil-streaked wings the central turret of a second Fortress was spitting flame at him from its twin machine-guns. Hans opened up his turbines to their fullest extent, twisted to avoid a collision with the Fort, slipped between two others, and skimmed past another, which was going down in a spin and trailing an enormous plume of black smoke. Finally he emerged out of the box, climbing vertically through a cloud of fighters which were totally incapable of catching him.

During those lively seconds he had lost sight of his companions. For a brief moment he caught sight of the familiar outline of a Messerschmitt 262 firing point-blank at a Fortress, which exploded in the air, dragging its neighbour down with it.

By now the impeccable box had become dislocated. From one bomber going down in flames on its back he saw half a dozen of the crew jump, while the planes behind shied aside hastily, so as not to ram or collapse the parachutes.

As he had some ammunition left, Hans attacked a second time, rather reluctantly. This time he chose the top layer of the first box, composed of Liberators. He aimed carefully at the one on the extreme right, making the little dot and the luminous cross of the gyroscopic sight coincide on his victim's fuselage. He then released the rest of his rockets in one long salvo.

With the Ez 42 it was impossible to miss! The Liberator, hit by several rockets, just disintegrated. Hans watched fascinated, at the same time moving out of range of the concerted fire of the hundreds of machine-guns. But he did not see the four Mustangs diving down at full throttle from immediately above him. The 262 shook from the impact of the .5-inch bullets. Hans broke so violently that the slots on his leading edge came open with a clang and con trails immediately formed on his wing-tips. He righted his plane as quickly as possible, but the A.S.I. had already passed the red mark at 600 m.p.h. and the Messerschmitt went into a convulsive pitching movement which hurled the pilot forward in spite of the tight straps of his safety-harness.

Hans only succeeded in stabilising the motion of his plane a full sixty miles from the fight. Exhausted by the effort, he looked at his gauges—only eighty gallons of fuel left, hardly five minutes' flying. He tried to call his Schwarmfuehrer, but his radio was dead, probably smashed by the Mustang's bullets. He would have to be quick to land by daylight, as the sun was already low over Denmark.

Hans got his bearings from the Weser and almost at once picked up Steinhuder Lake. Only three minutes now to his base.

Going into a shallow dive he throttled back to 6500 revs, as one turbine was overheating. He was safe now, but that and the thought of his two successes failed to make him feel good. Those successes felt almost like defeats—they might be the last—and everything that he had built his life on was collapsing like a house of cards.

Immediately over Steinhuder he flattened out at 2500 feet, throttling back to 3000 revs. The airfield must be quite close now, probably to the right of the blazing fires in Hanover.

350 m.p.h.—he put down 10 degrees of flap to reduce speed still more and get his undercart down. The runway at Langenhagen stretched between the ruins and the charred pine-trees. Not a soul. How different from his first trips in Libya. Nobody left to help him down from the cockpit and congratulate him. No celebrations in the Mess round the newly broached barrel of beer. Would he even find somewhere to sleep free from the nightmare of being pulverised by a deluge of bombs?

He pushed down the undercart lever and waited for the three separate jolts that would tell him that each wheel had locked . . . thud . . . one . . . thud . . . two . . . suddenly the whole world exploded before his eyes, a blinding flash as a shell smashed his instrument panel and a sudden pain as splinters lashed into his legs. Dead silence for a fraction of a second, then a terrific explosion as one turbine burst, tearing the wing off. The Messerschmitt turned over. Hans fumbled for the button of the seat-ejector mechanism, but his wounded arm was glued to his side by the centrifugal force. A second jolt as the other wing broke off. The earth rose straight up in front of him.

Hans knew this was the end. He seemed quite calm. Yet in the Hitler Jugend they had not taught him to pray.

In the shooting-box they had followed the unfolding of the drama, and they had all instinctively winced when the Messer-schmitt hit the ground. It was only then that they saw the two R.A.F. Tempests, shooting like arrows up into the low clouds. Why had the flak not opened up? Night began to creep up the hillside.

In 1938, shortly after the Bayerische Flugzeugwerke had been taken over by its technical director, Willy Messerschmitt, and had assumed his name, the company began working on the design of a jet-propelled fighter.

Messerschmitt wanted a very fast plane, capable of outdistancing enemy fighters. He therefore evolved a slender, beautifully balanced swept wing, and fitted it to a pear-shaped fuselage. The first prototype flew with a Jumo 211 mounted in the nose and driving an air-screw, since the new turbo-jets were not sufficiently developed. That was early in 1940.

In 1941 Heinkel-Hirth He 58 jet units became available, but gave so little thrust that the new fighters were unable to get off the ground.

Nearly two years elapsed before the Junkers engineers came along with a new turbo-jet unit. It was the Jumo 004A. Here at last was the solution of Messerschmitt's problem.

He slung two of these jets under his wing, and tapered his fuselage to a perfectly stream-lined nose, in which he mounted four 30-mm. cannon.

On the 3rd January 1942 the Messerschmitt 262 jet flew for the first time. It did not have a tricycle undercarriage at that time, and taking off turned out to be a perilous business, the jet streams flinging large chunks of concrete and earth about.

Later prototypes flew, with tricycle undercarriages, and immediately showed phenomenal speed. The Ministry, however, was not interested and the prototype, though it continued its tests, sank back into obscurity.

In the end the weight of American daylight bombing over Germany forced General der Flieger Galland to take up the question again and an initial series was ordered. Unfortunately Hitler saw a demonstration of the plane, was very impressed and decided to use it as a bomber for reprisals against England. It was one of Hitler's 'irrevocable' decisions and Goering did not dare oppose it. However, after six months' argument and discussion, Galland persuaded Hitler to change his mind.

Messerschmitt 262s began to come off the assembly line and by November 1944 four squadrons were equipped with them. Goering never forgave Galland and had him replaced by Gollob.

Gollob, besides being a firm believer in the Messerschmitt 262, was a superb fighter-pilot and an outstanding engineer. He speeded up production and worked hard at perfecting the armament.

The Messerschmitt 262, the first jet fighter to be used in battle, revolutionised aerial warfare. If it had not been for the six months lost through Hitler's interference it would have reversed the situation in the skies over Europe.

The Messerschmitt 262, with a total power of 2600-lb. static thrust, had in 1944 the same speed as the F-84 Thunderjet with 5000-lb. thrust today. It had a margin of speed of more than 120 m.p.h. over the most up-to-date fighters possessed by the Allies at that time. Its armament, four 30-mm. cannon, was formidable.

The colossal amount of work that had gone into the design

and production of the plane can be gauged by the fact that it incorporated developments which even now cause American, British and French engineers to scratch their heads. Special parachute harness with portable oxygen-bottle for baling out at high speeds and great-heights. Angle of incidence of tailplane adjustable during flight to change the plane's trim at supersonic speeds; swept wing; multiple ailerons and servo-operated controls; self-ejecting seat; gyroscopic sight; radar; air-to-air rockets, etc. There was even a two-seater radar version, i.e. an all-weather fighter.

Gollob's use of anti-aircraft rockets on the Messerschmitt 262 was a bold leap into the future—just how bold can be judged by the fact that in 1950 the Americans were still using .5 machine-guns. In a few years' time someone will no doubt re-invent the R4M, although it had reached perfection in 1945. The Russians have been quicker off the mark.

Luckily for the Allies, Messerschmitt 262s equipped with the Gollob combination of Ez 42 sight, R4M rocket and 30-mm. cannon were only used on one occasion. When our troops got to Lübeck the R.W. factory was producing 25,000 R4Ms a month, but the Messerschmitt 262 assembly plant had been pulverised. As for the Messerschmitts already on squadron, they were immobilised from March 1945 by lack of spares and also by the very close watch kept on the airfields from which they operated.

In spite of everything, about four hundred Messerschmitt 262s were used in combat and the Allies found them a considerable nuisance, in spite of their superiority in numbers.

The dimensions and performance figures of the Messerschmitt 262 were as follows: wing-span 41 feet, length 35 feet, wing area 234 square feet, total weight 8 tons. Maximum speed over 560 m.p.h, Take-off run with 12 m.p.h. head-wind, nearly 1100 yards.

CHAPTER NINE

UNDER THE SIGN OF THE DIVINE WIND

The Japanese Kamikaze[15] suicide-planes were to bring a curious medieval touch of savagery not unmixed with nobility into the Pacific campaigns of 1944-45. The origin of the name Kamikaze has to be sought in the folklore of Japan, in the naïve and impassioned chronicles of her heroic antiquity.

In 1223 the Mongol invasion of Kubla Khan swept over China, which was quickly submerged. The cruel Tartar's spies were not long in bringing news of the snow-flanked volcanoes and flower gardens of the Yasukina Isles, a country of tranquil beauty and peace.

In 1285 the massed fleet of junks, collected from the rivers and coasts of China, carried the terrible warriors to Formosa. When the smoke from the ravaged homesteads cleared, there were the blue islands etched against the horizon.

In 1281 the invasion fleet was sailing towards Japan when it was dispersed and annihilated by the sacred tornado unleashed by Tenshi, the Son of Heaven. The Nipponese Islands were saved. This was Kamikaze, the Divine Wind.

---

[15] The Kamikaze is the commonest name and was the only one used by the Allies. The Japanese did, however, use other names, including Tokkotai, Shinshu and Kamiwashi. Formosa pilots used the term Makoto, and those from Kyushu used Shimbu, a word meaning 'brave.'

The Allies first learned the significance of this word in tragic circumstances, at the time of the Leyte landings in autumn 1944.

It was under this name that special units of volunteers were formed, men who undertook to crash their bomb-loaded planes on to American ships. In this war of modern technical weapons, of complex amphibious operations utilising every resource of science, radar, and even the first guided missiles, reports on the Kamikazes were at first received with polite incredulity. Yet what if they were true!

Our civilised conscience could accept total sacrifice in its noblest form, in the heat of battle or in a paroxysm of suffering or despair—Max Guedj in Norway; Lieutenant Keenan, mortally wounded, crashing his fighter on the torpedo that was going to blow up his ship. Or else in connection with desperate missions where pilots were pretty well certain they would never return, but where nevertheless the element of chance or superhuman skill might succeed in cheating the rules of probability—the Fairey Battles at Maestricht in 1940, for example. And I am certain that at such moments a glimmer of hope still burned, however faintly, in the hearts of those men.

We have also seen the generous and heroic impulse of the man who covers his chief's body with his own so as to receive the bullet himself—Maridor, for instance, hurling his Spitfire XIV into the VI diving on the hospital, or Thomas Mansergh, V.C., remaining at the controls of his blazing Stirling to allow his crew to bale out.

On the other hand, the psychology of the Kamikaze pilots, with its complete detachment, its total disdain of death, its monstrous cold-bloodedness, is hard for a European to grasp, and harder still for an American. It is not only too easy but also quite erroneous to explain it all away on the basis of some vague 'Oriental fatalism'. This attitude, with which the Japanese are often credited, is the exact opposite of the principle which motivated these special units of the Imperial Air Force. They were the instrument by which destiny was to be reversed and the implacable logic of military rules broken.

In war fatalism is passive. The Japanese showed us the value of passive resignation when their troops underwent crushing bombardments on Pacific atolls. The weight of explosive poured in one week on some troop positions on Tarawa, day and night, makes the most concentrated artillery hammering at Verdun look like chicken-feed. And yet immediately afterwards the attacking troops were met with fanatical resistance. A normal European soldier would have been driven out of his mind, and lost all will to fight.

Then what is the explanation? It is not too easy to find.

Shintoism, the national religion of the Japanese, had been re-established in all its pomp by the Mikados at the time of the restoration. This religion, based on a legendary explanation of the birth of the world, affirmed the divinity of the Mikado and, by extension, of his people and his empire. This mystical belief, sublimated in Bushido, the warriors' creed, was in keeping with the aspirations of the Samurai caste and the military class. The Divine Empire's political aim, the unification of the eight corners of the world under one roof—Hakko Ishui—was the direct consequence.

The warrior who sacrificed himself in the interests of this *mystique* took his place among the divine hierarchy according to a complex code of honour. A moral system based on blind and unconditional devotion to the fatherland as incarnated in the person of the Emperor was bound to produce fanatics. So, when the Japanese military were forced to admit American material superiority and saw their visions fade of offering the Emperor absolute hegemony over the Pacific, the rules of Bushido imposed suicide on them. Only hara-kiri could expiate their fault and save face. So it was that the Kamikaze idea was born, early in 1944.

At first, contrary to what Allied propaganda led us to believe, those who came forward were mostly from among the most highly cultured Japanese, and there was certainly more en-thusiasm for this weapon among the higher officers and the survivors of the regular Air Force than among the middle-class conscripted pilots. In any case, hara-kiri and other forms of ritual suicide were the prerogative of the nobles and the ruling classes.

Kamikaze thus became what might be called a utilitarian form of hara-kiri practised by the Imperial Air Force. It must also be admitted that the leaders of a race which had produced the *Yamato*[16] and the Zero had a shrewd idea of the practical value suicide-planes would have. They were the first to set the example.

---

[16] The *Yamato* and her sister-ship the *Musashi* were the two most powerful warships in the world, more powerful even than the *Tirpitz* or the *Bismarck*. They displaced 75,000 tons (the *Vanguard* displaces 42,500 tons), had a speed of 30 knots, and had nine 16-inch guns, plus formidable secondary armament. Both were sunk by air attack.

This was not the Greek philosopher drinking hemlock, or the vanquished Roman general falling on his sword. It was the soldier, not only saving face and his own honour, but also bringing the benefit of this act to the service of his country. The symbolic Bushido gesture quickly became a frightening weapon of war.

* * *

Major Katushige Takata of the Imperial Army Air Force was the first to perform a deliberate Kamikaze. At Biak on 17th May 1944 he hurled his Zero upon an American destroyer, killing twenty-three men and causing the loss of the ship through fire.

A few days later a Naval Air Force officer, Lieutenant Kobi, crashed his twin-engined Betty, carrying two torpedoes with contact fuses, into the side of a British aircraft-carrier in the Indian Ocean.

There had previously been some isolated cases—in the naval battles round Guadalcanal particularly—of pilots whose planes were in flames or too badly damaged to return to base, ramming American ships. But those could be put down to outbursts of rage or hatred and were not the result of a preconceived and carefully executed plan.

The Kamikaze idea fired public opinion in Japan. The enthusiasm, sedulously fostered by propaganda, reached to our eyes fantastic proportions. The candidates were to all intents and purposes deified, and honours and large pensions were bestowed upon their descendants. Clothed in ceremonial black or white robes, purified by invocations to the gods, their heads carefully shaved, they were the subject of positive worship by the populace before they joined their special units.

In July 1944 seventeen units were formed, each equipped with twelve Zero (Zeke 52) fighters with two 500-lb. bombs clamped under the wings. Fourteen of these units, mostly Naval Air Force ones, were sent to the Philippines when the American invasion was threatening. Via Singapore, they came down towards the Sunda Islands, finally establishing their bases on the airfields at Dulag, Tacloban and Tolosa, on Leyte.

Their opportunity was not long in coming. On 13th October the American Fleet under Admiral Halsey entered Leyte Gulf through the straits of Surigao. At dawn on 14th October Vice-Admiral Masabumi Arima personally led three Kamikaze squadrons into the attack. One hour later he crashed his plane on to the deck of the aircraft-carrier *Hornet,* while his thirty-five pilots made their own choice among the other ships—and there were plenty to choose from. When it was all over, the. last plane down and the last A.A. shell fired, the *Hornet* limped away, and had to be withdrawn from service for the time being. The aircraft-carriers *Franklin* and *Hancock* were hit and suffered numerous casualties, as did the *Reno.* Three troopships and the cruiser *Houston* were sunk.

By the end of 1944 the fourteen units had accomplished their task with impressive success. On 21st November, for instance, Tokyo radio announced that the Kamikazes would prevent the cruiser *Nashville,* carrying MacArthur's staff, from leaving Philippine waters. On 13th December one single crafty Kamikaze, ignoring the concentrated A.A. of the entire naval squadron, calmly identified his objective and planted himself on the *Nashville's* bridge at 550 m.p.h. Result, 127 killed, 163 wounded. Admiral Strubble escaped by a miracle; he was hurled against a door by the blast, but got off with a broken rib; General Drunkel and Colonels Muthe and Monrisey were put *hors de combat.*

The operation against the naval convoy off Lingayen was carried out by the last four Kamikaze squadrons. They arrived over the target mingled with orthodox bombers. As a result the A.A. failed to pick them out and in the confusion five ships were sunk and twenty-five badly and forty-two slightly damaged. A total of 1600 American soldiers and sailors were killed.

It was terrifying, and the American Navy rather lost that feeling of being on top which it had acquired after its recent victories. Draconion measures were taken by the censorship to prevent the Japanese from getting to know the damage they had done. Unfortunately the jungle-covered islands swarmed with spies in enemy pay, and Tokyo was soon informed.

The Japanese now started doing the thing in a big way. On Kyushu, the most southerly of the main Japanese islands, the suicide-planes began to mass on the airfields. And, not content with using normal fighters and bombers, they decided to create a special machine for the job. Hence the Oka or Baka.[17]

It was a single-seater plane in miniature, rocket-propelled and reaching 600 m.p.h. and carrying a one-ton warhead in the nose.

---

[17] Oka was the Japanese name, which meant 'thunderclap.' The Americans called them Baka, meaning 'madman', and they are usually known under this name.

The designer of this piloted flying-bomb was Captain Niki. It was brought to within about twenty-five miles of the objective—i.e. still out of range of A.A. guns—by a parent plane. Owing to its speed, this machine was virtually unstoppable, and it could cause appalling damage, as the Americans were soon to discover.

The island of Onkinawa marked the last step before the invasion of the Japanese mainland, and its strategic importance justified sacrifices. However, after the Iwo Jima business in February 1945—this mere pimple on the ocean had cost the Marines 20,616 lives before they captured it—the American staff had decided to leave nothing to chance. A formidable armada consisting of 318 warships and 1119 transports carrying 548,000 men appeared on the morning of 1st April off this little island, hardly as big as the Isle of Wight.

After eighty-two days of bitter, ferocious fighting Okinawa fell. But in the meantime the Kamikazes had struck. Result:

33 warships sunk, including some aircraft-carriers and cruisers.

57 transports lost.

223 ships damaged.

12,260 men killed.

33,769 men wounded.

The Japanese lost 2702 planes, normal and suicide, in that battle. Most of the stocks of Bakas were immobilised on the island itself, luckily for the Americans. Some were used for the first time in the massed attack on 12th April. Out of 38 launched, 13 scored hits and destroyed their targets.

Overwhelmed by this avalanche, the U.S. Navy sent back

desperate SOS's for immediate supplies of special A.A. ammunition and replacements of 20- and 40-mm. gun barrels. Hundreds of tons of shells with proximity fuses were sent out from the States by air to stop the rot.

In fact, this was only the beginning of the battle. Okinawa was now the jumping-off point for the invasion of Japan. Thousands of ships were concentrating there, thousands of tons of supplies were piling up. The Kamikazes—there were about 2000 of them scattered among the thirty-three main airfields on Kyushu—continued their daily attacks on this enormous target where every hit was a bull.

To reduce the extent of the destruction the Americans took sweeping measures. The island was ringed by about a hundred radar-equipped destroyers. They could call into action 625 fighter planes and 7400 A.A. guns controlled by 140 radar posts. Under this umbrella of steel the preparations went on, but so did the damage. Fourteen of the destroyers were sunk and forty-two damaged by Kamikazes. The *Laffey* alone was attacked eighty-four times in one day. She was hit ten times, destroyed twenty-three aircraft, and dodged the rest. After a couple of days fifty of the crew had to be evacuated, suffering from shattered nervous systems. It was hardly surprising.

* * *

On 6th August 1945 at 1.45 a.m. Superfortress No. 44-86292 took off from Tinian airfield. Its pilot Lieutenant-Col. Paul Tibbetts, had christened his big four-engined plane 'Enola Gay' in honour of his mother. At 8.15 a.m. the lone aircraft opened its specially constructed bomb-bay. A long, dark shape, checked by a small parachute, spiralled down in the sunny summer sky over Hiroshima. It was the first atomic bomb.

* * *

9th August 1945

The great naval air-base at Omura, the oldest and also the most important on Kyushu as its planes covered the naval yards at Sasebo and Nagasaki, was nothing but a heap of ruins. The position of the five great runways could only be distinguished by the different colour of the craters. The airfield was pitted all over with them, mostly brown ringed with red earth. But where the runways had been they were grey and bespattered with pale lumps of concrete. Aircraft were still burning, mere shells— Zeros, Norms, Sallys, slender-nosed Nicks, tubby Jacks, twin-engined Helens. Smashed fuselages, duralumin plates sawn in half by machine-gun bullets, smashed undercarts, black remains of burnt-out engines, propellers twisted into pathetic shapes, puddles of molten aluminium under collapsed wings. A blanket of heavy oil smoke drifting towards the sea covered this charnel-house.

The hangars and workshops had been razed to the ground and the debris scattered far and wide by blast. Yet some men had survived the cataclysm. They swarmed over the field, collecting what was still usable, rolling drums of petrol, unearthing ammunition boxes from caches covered with dry grass.

Within the gaping foundations of the control tower a shelter had been rigged up with camouflaged tarpaulins. In one corner stood a long telescopic wireless aerial flanked by an improvised chimney. Four men sat there in silence.

The first was crouched down and with rapid strokes of his fan was brightening a small charcoal fire and watching some salmon balls cooking. A second, kneeling on the lowest step of the stairs, was rolling more balls between his fingers. The ground was littered with empty tins, a few bottles of Saki and cigarette butts. On the wall, hanging on nails, were a few oil-stained flying-suits, helmets and oxygen masks.

Sitting back to back on the edge of a table covered with naval charts the two other men were listening to Tokyo radio:

'Hiroshima . . . dead too numerous to count . . . inhabitants burnt alive in the streets or crushed under collapsing houses . . . impossible to distinguish the dead from the wounded . . . impossible to identify them . . . honourable peace . . . new weapon and flames from the sky . . . honourable peace . . . honourable peace . . .'[18]

The transmission was poor and the speaker's voice was interrupted by interference. But the sense was clear enough. It was a call to capitulate.

The man nearest the radio stretched out his arm and turned it off and turned towards his companion. His lips in a thin line, the latter was abstractedly toying with his Samurai sword, drawing the gleaming blade from the brown lacquer scabbard and ramming it

---

[18] These were the very terms used in the second broadcast from Tokyo radio announcing the dropping of the atomic bomb on Hiroshima.

home again with his gloved palm. Both were in the black uniform of the Imperial Navy. On the collar of his tunic one had a gold star. He was Rear-Admiral Ugaki, commanding the fifth air fleet; the other had two stars. He was Vice-Admiral Fukada, commanding the first mobile detachment of the Naval Air Force.

Their units were now scattered over the devastated airfields of the island of Kyushu and there was no possibility of re-establishing control. There they were in that shelter, their commands had dwindled away and there was no hope left. The moment had come, the moment they had so often discussed as they drank their green tea. There was only one honourable way out.

Looking long into each other's eyes, without saying a word, according to the customary farewell as between brothers in arms, they bowed low. They then exchanged swords after kissing the ivory hilts, and bowed again. How far off were the happy days when, as young cadets, they had parcelled up the world every evening and offered it to their Emperor. A brief order, and the two orderlies ran up the stairs. From outside came the sound of shouts and men running. The two admirals sat down again, facing each other this time, and heads bowed and arms crossed they meditated in silence.

* * *

Hundreds of men on the airfield were converging on the narrow road which led to the cliffs. They swarmed down the steps cut in the rock. Down below the placid waters of Sasebo Bay lapped the gently sloping beach.

The men swept away with brooms the inch or two of carefully raked sand which hid a long runway built of planks. They removed the camouflage nets draping the rocks, revealing caves at the foot of the cliffs. Cormorants used to disport themselves there, but the men had enlarged the caves with picks and dynamite and they now sheltered a few precious planes still remaining.

Two Bettys were laboriously trundled out by the sweating men, the wheels sinking in the sand. The lowering storm-laden sky hung like a pall in the heavy electric heat.

The mechanics started up the engines at once. There were no starter batteries. Instead they used a curious system of ropes wound round the airscrew spinner. Three men gave a sudden heave, and the perfectly serviced Kasei 21 in each case started straight away, throwing back a cloud of sand which scraped off the paint on the tailplane like emery paper.

The crews arrived. The pilots wore thick pebble glasses and moved clumsily in their sheepskin jackets.

A Lilliputian tractor emerged from a tunnel, dragging two trailers. On each was a Baka, carefully laid in a padded cradle. The armourers brought out trolleys carrying one-ton cylinders of T.N.T., which they fitted into the nose of the machines with the help of the tackle on the tractor. The five detonators were carefully screwed home and the whole covered by a streamlined nose.

The engines were now warm and so they were switched off. The Bakas were slipped under the Bettys' bellies, between the legs of the undercarriage. Everything was all set. There must have been upwards of a thousand men round the planes, their eyes fixed on the stairway hewn in the cliff.

Admirals Ugaki and Fukada slowly descended the steps. Ugaki had slipped on over his uniform a long white robe, with the sleeves turned up to the elbows. On the back was embroidered a five-petalled pink cherry blossom, and the same emblem was painted on the fuselage of the two Bakas. Fukada had simply thrown a sort of white cape over his shoulders and he held a Samurai sword clasped against his chest with both hands.

It was exactly 11.02 a.m. Everyone bowed low before the two officers, and at that very moment a vivid flash ripped the sky, so brilliant that the clouds were still shimmering with light a long time afterwards. The men straightened up with a jerk, and before their terrified gaze a colossal pillar of flame rose up behind the green hills on the other side of the bay. It rose, incredibly wide, straight towards the sky. They knew that at the foot of that dazzling column, which surged up dragging with it billowing white and pink clouds of vapour, stood Nagasaki.

Four prodigious thunderclaps rolled from hill to hill like an earthquake. Stones broke away from the cliff. In spite of the distance, a sudden gust, like the wind from a gigantic fan, whipped up the water and swept ribbons of foam over the bay. Enormous balls of fire burgeoned and were swept up by the air rising from the flames into the incandescent clouds. Others and yet others bellied out and pursued them upwards. The sky now was as heavy as lead, except over there where the fires of Nagasaki formed a monstrous false dawn.

197

It had all been so quick, and so unreal, that they stood transfixed with horror. They would have remained petrified
indefinitely, but the blast of a whistle broke the silence. The men
bestirred themselves and returned to their tasks, but they kept
on turning to look towards the south.

After a last accolade the two admirals, assisted by the respect-
ful ground-crews, took their place in the exiguous cockpits of the
Bakas. They tightened the safety straps and the transparent
hoods were carefully screwed down over their heads. A hook was
inserted into the ring on either side of the cockpit and the winch
jerkily heaved up each flying-torpedo until it was wedged against
the Betty's fuselage. Four steel braces kept them rigidly in place.

Ugaki, enclosed in that aluminium and perspex coffin, was
already cut off from his fellow men. He was in darkness, for the
Baka's cockpit fitted tightly into the plane's bomb-bay. The two
rudders of his machine pressed like hands against the cold round
belly of the Betty. The voices from outside came muffled through
the walls of his plane as from another world. He felt the slight jolts
as the crew climbed on board. The door opening cast a brief ray of
light and he saw for one moment the copper wires and tubes criss-
crossing, like entrails stuck on the smooth walls of the plane's
abdomen. He felt the shudder as the engines started up, heard the
radar antennae vibrate in harmony with the whirring propellers.
By pressing his cheek against the perspex, Ugaki could cast a
glance downwards. He saw only the planks of the runway
trembling under the oleo-legs. A brake squeaked, then another as
the pilot lined the aircraft up. The throb of the engines ticking over
gave way to a roar as they opened up and the Betty began to move.

As he was suspended slightly behind the centre of gravity, he felt, amplified, the pilot's kicks on the rudder bar to correct incipient swings. Spurts of sand grated on the Baka's stubby wings.

There was a crosswind and the take-off seemed to take ages. The plane bounced clumsily on one wheel. Ugaki felt a twinge of anxiety, not for himself, as he had already ceased to be, but an accident now would mean that his mission had failed.

The jolting ceased. The plane lurched in the air, as the pilot tried to steady it for the climb. As the flaps were raised, the airflow seemed to press him into the body of the aircraft. The wheels shuddered as they were still revolving when the under-cart came up, then he felt the plane beginning to climb. The thin metal skin quivered in the airflow.

Now it was just a question of waiting. In about 150 minutes the green light would come on, meaning he must get ready. Then the red light and he would be dropped, facing the enemy. Until then he would be left hunched up, alone, with his thoughts. Only the slow, desperately slow, luminous hands of his watch linked him with the outside world.

It was 11.50. Two Myrts[19] must by now have joined the two Bettys, taking off from one of the three airfields at Kumamoto. They belonged to the 18th Flotilla and each had been fitted to carry a 22-in. torpedo. Who would be flying them? The officers must have thrown dice for the honour of participating in this mission.

---

[19] See note at end of chapter.

12 o'clock.—The Hondo archipelago, a rocky tracery strewn over the China sea, where the multi-coloured junks and sampans with their sails of straw glide on the sunlit waters. He quickly suppressed a poignant regret.

12.10.—They must be over Kagashima Bay with its moving sands criss-crossed with palisades where the pearl oysters are patiently cultivated. Dirty yellow waters, the home of the giant ray, that offspring of the devil.

12.15.—Above Kanoya airfield the escort of George[20] fighters climbed to join them, circling like vultures. They were to protect them as far as Okinawa. How many intact planes would they have succeeded in collecting?

Nearly two interminable hours had now dragged by. Cramp knotted his thighs. The oxygen was beginning to run short—after the bombardment there had been no equipment at Omura for recharging the bottles. The cold, too, penetrated the thin cloth of his uniform. There was nothing to be seen down below, the dazzling sunlight blotted everything out.

The parent plane, handicapped by the extra drag of the Baka, was beginning to labour. Ugaki could feel by its sluggishness that it had reached its ceiling—about 23,000 feet. The engines were doing their best, but their unsteady, fluctuating beat showed that the pilot was having a job synchronising them.

1.40.—Green light! Ugaki planted his feet firmly on the rudder bar and took a firm grip on the stick with one hand and on the trimmer with the other. His body was tensed forward. What was

---

[20] See note at end of chapter.

there inside that shaven head under the black leather helmet? Hatred? Cold rage? Fear of the unknown? Probably a deliberate blank. The thoughts which are life to us were merely incidental to him, banished by concentration on the act he still had to accomplish.

1.41.—Red! The braces parted with a twang and the Baka fell into space. The sudden sunlight seared his eyeballs. Made nose-heavy by the weight of its warhead, the machine immediately went into a dive. A gently left-right movement to get the feel of the controls—the Baka was horribly unstable. A glance at the instrument panel: A.S.I. 360 m.p.h.; altimeter 23,000 feet; artificial horizon, nose low; compass, heading South.

On the left, the selector box for the five rocket units—two under the wings and three in the fuselage. Then, straight in front, the red-painted arming handle. He gave it a sharp pull. The trinitro-anisol charge was now live. His thumb pressed the button on the stick and the wing rockets came into action. Ugaki was glued to his seat, his back bent by the terrific acceleration. 530 m.p.h., but he had already lost 3000 precious feet of altitude. He glanced round. Far behind him the Bettys were turning for home. The two Myrts were diving vertically down covered by the Georges. Down below lay the semi-circle of destroyers, like bright needles on the blue sea, forming the radar screen for Okinawa straight ahead.

The island seemed to float like the corpse of some deep-sea monster. Only the thin reptilian backbone emerged, scarred with the straight lines of the eight American landing-strips. Right at the tip stood Mount Kuribare, with its dark gaping crater, overlooking Bruckner Bay, which was swarming with ships.

The ear-splitting sound of the rockets had alerted the batteries at Ie Shima, but this flying torpedo was going so fast that the A.A. burst far behind its fiery wake. To the left, followed by black bursts from 40-mm. fire and white bursts from 20-mm., Fukada's Baka was hurtling like a meteor down towards the Kyukyu roadstead.

Behind him the two Myrts, two slender cruciform shapes, followed at water level. A first explosion—a hit—then a spout of water near a Liberty ship—a miss.

Admiral Ugaki was already over the island. It was nothing but a burnt shell, gashed by the zigzags of the trenches and pitted with bomb craters so close together that they overlapped. Not a tree, not a speck of green left. The bulldozers were pushing up mounds of earth to block the entrances of underground shelters where whole companies of Japanese soldiers had been burnt alive by flame-throwers. Already the smoke-pots on the shore were beginning to vomit a thick protective screen, swept and scattered over Bruckner Bay by the violent wind. But it was too late, and the anchored fleet, lit up with the flashes from the guns, was putting up an umbrella of explosives and steel.

The Baka, now at only 5000 feet, skimmed the sides of Mount Kuribare, where burnt-out shells of tanks still lay among the streams of lava.

At last, the objective. The anchorage was fringed with the gaping hulls of grounded ships—the work of Kamikazes. What would be a target worthy of the sacrifice? The cruisers with their slender funnels? The South Dakota class battleships? There were three of these at anchor, squatting on their antitorpedo bulges.

Or, better still, the big, square aircraft-carriers, with their lop-sided superstructure.

His mind was made up. He fired his last three rockets and at 600 m.p.h., like a comet dragging its fiery trail, the Baka bore down upon the biggest of the carriers.

The steel ring of his rudimentary sight encircled the medley of platforms forming the control tower on the side of the flight-deck. The Baka was so fast that all he saw of the ships he skimmed past was the flashes from their A.A. batteries. He dived through a tunnel of tracer and passed between a double row of spurts cutting up the sea.

Ugaki was now skimming a few feet above the water. The enormous grey mass rose up and towered above him. Only a few yards now—men running—shells converging on him from forty guns—rows of rivets showing on the hull.

He squared his shoulders, shouting Banzai! Before the Sun of death he had not blenched.

At a speed of nearly 1000 feet a second the Baka had per-forated the hull and exploded in No. 2 hangar of the *Savo Island.*

The blast had piled the twenty-odd planes inside the hangar into a crushed heap, together with the men working on them. A flood of burning petrol engulfed everything. Luckily the plane-lift was down, otherwise the imprisoned gases would have burst the ship. As it was, they escaped through the gaping hole. The pumps swamped the burning hangar with carbonic foam and saved the aircraft-carrier.

Thirty-nine men were killed and many others knocked out by the shock. When the fire was out, all they found of the Baka and its pilot were the arming-vanes of the percussion cap, a few scraps of twisted metal and a Samurai sword. Inside the charred sheath the blade was intact.

While this drama unfolded, the twelve faithful Georges had come down with the two Myrts in their final dive. Afterwards they had climbed again at full throttle, only to be set upon immediately by thirty P-5 Is, joined almost at once by twenty-four P-47s. Fifty-four to twelve—the pendulum had swung back a long way since Bataan!

Thanks to their superior manoeuvrability, four Georges succeeded in getting away, while the others succumbed to sheer numbers. The four survivors, faster than the P-5 Is, regrouped over the sea and, in perfect formation, made straight for a large transport which was preparing to enter Kyuku roads. The American A.A. did not shoot, thinking they were P-47s, which were very similar in appearance.

The 2500 tons of explosives in the ship's holds produced an absolute tidal wave.

So ended the last Kamikaze mission of the war.

* * *

The next day the Domei agency announced that Japan was laying down arms according to the terms of the Potsdam declaration, with a proviso concerning the spiritual authority of the Emperor. On 15th August President Truman officially confirmed the end of hostilities.

More even than by the atomic bomb the Japanese had been crushed by American air power in the Pacific. The American Army and Navy Air Forces, more or less wiped out in the initial assault, had quickly been built up again. The Army Air Force on 1st January 1943 had 1622 combat planes and 91,600 men in the Pacific. In 1944 these figures were 3174 planes and 245,077 men. On 1st January 1945 it had 4911 planes and 402,406 men, and this reached, on 1st August 1945, a total of 7260 planes and 467,957 men.

The Naval Air Force expanded from 127 planes on 10th December 1941 to 14,648 planes on 1st August 1945.

The Japanese Air Forces had 2520 front-line planes and 78,520 men in January 1942; 3200 planes and 84,500 men in January 1943; 4050 planes and 117,000 men in January 1944; 4150 planes and 184,250 men in January 1945. Finally, on the day of the Armistice there were left 4600 front-line planes, plus about 5000 planes modified for Kamikaze work.

General Kawabe, director for Kamikaze operations in the Imperial G.H.Q., later declared before an American court of enquiry:

'We do not wish you to describe the Kamikaze tactics as suicide-attacks. The Kamikaze pilot regarded himself as a human bomb which was going to destroy a unit of the fleet attacking his country. He derived glory from it. I do not believe that these methods materially contributed towards our defeat. Right up to the end we thought we could counterbalance your material and scientific strength with our spiritual convictions and our moral strength.

'Whatever you may think about the Kamikazes, you can be certain that the pilots died happy, in the firm conviction that their sacrifice was one more step towards the Emperor's victory.'

How can one answer a declaration of that sort? Our European minds are just baffled.

However, on 9th August 1945, Admiral Ugaki and Admiral Fukada did not die for victory. They died because they did not want to survive defeat, and that, for the first time, brings their gesture within the scope of our comprehension.

Notes on the Baka, the German 'Natter', the Myrt and the George

At both ends of the earth the disproportion of strength and the growing shadow of defeat forced Japanese and German engineers into a desperate search for defensive weapons.

The Japanese problem was how to stop the American Navy and prevent it getting close to Japan. Only the most extreme measures could be of any avail. After using normal aircraft on Kamikaze missions, the next step was logically—if that is the right word—to build special machines still better adapted for this blood-curdling sport. The result was the Baka, whose main characteristics are made clear in the previous chapter.

The feature about this machine which strikes the European most forcibly is that once the pilot was inside and it had been hoisted into the parent plane's bomb-bay, it was impossible for him to change his mind and get out.

The Baka pilot only had four instruments: an air-speed indicator, an altimeter, an artificial horizon and a compass. Although the control surfaces were very small, the pilot had to exert considerable muscular strength to manoeuvre his plane owing to the speed at which it flew. In addition, the total duration of its flight was only five minutes or so—representing a range of only forty miles—so that the pilot had a very short time to get his machine under control and lined-up on the objective. Furthermore, the last six miles were flown at a speed approaching that of sound, which again complicated the pilot's task. As a result, only the most experienced pilots were entrusted with these highly tricky machines.

The first 300 Bakas were stored in the underground hangars on Okinawa, and the Japanese, who were taken by surprise by the American landings, could neither use them nor evacuate them—a lucky break for the U.S. Navy!

They continued to be produced on Kyushu, but the end was drawing near. About 150 were used, and only a rather small proportion—about 30 per cent.—scored hits.

The prototype of a Baka which could take off under its own power, by means of five solid-explosive rockets and two German Walter rockets, was found in the naval depot at Yokusoka.

The German problem was not dissimilar. It consisted in stopping the R.A.F. and U.S.A.F. heavy bombers. Heinkel, Messerschmitt, Junkers and Bachem all submitted proposals. Bachem's was the one to be taken up. His solution seems so fantastic, even today, that it gives any normal pilot an icy shiver down his spine. It was the BP 'Natter', or 'viper'. The Natter was

16 feet long, had a wing-span of 10 feet and a wing area of 60 square feet. The power unit was a Walter Hwk 509 rocket developing a 3700-lb. thrust for four minutes. Climbing vertically, the Natter could reach 500 m.p.h., and when straight and level it touched 600 m.p.h.

Once the pilot was strapped into the tiny cockpit, the contraption was mounted on a vertical catapult and fired by means of two powder rockets when the enemy bombers were a few miles distant. Within a few seconds the pilot was within range, or that was the idea anyway. All he had to do was get a Flying Fortress bang in front of him, and let fly with the twenty R4M rockets in the nose of his machine. This should pulverise the Fortress. Then the pilot pressed a button, detonating two explosive charges, whereupon the Natter broke into two pieces, ejecting the pilot on one parachute and the Walter rocket on another. Not an everyday idea, exactly.

The first test model—how on earth could people be found to take this sort of thing on!—did not stand up to the acceleration and the machine did a loop on take-off and crashed at 600 m.p.h. The pilot, according to the phrase current among fighter pilots, received a synthetic funeral.

The second took off all right, but he failed to get out and was killed. So was the third. Luckily for the fourth the Armistice arrived.

Ten or so complete 'Natters' were captured by the Allies, and the Americans tried to make two captured German test-pilots repeat the experiment, at Muroc in the U.S.A. As can be imagined, they refused politely, and every argument failed, from friendly persuasion and promises, via appeals to national pride, to threats of forced labour. One can sympathise.

One radio-controlled 'Natter' was launched, got out of hand, and crashed on a drug-store in Las Vegas. Energetic protests came from the inhabitants and the Press, and that was the end of the Bachem experiment.

The Saiun—American code-name 'Myrt'—was a development of the type which the firm of Nakajima had specialised in; a fast single-engined plane operating from aircraft-carriers and with a crew of either two or three. It was a development of the Kate and the Jill, which had been very successful in torpedo attacks during the battles of Guadalcanal and Midway.

The Myrt was also used by the Navy as a reconnaissance plane, by reason of its speed and its wide range. It was a single-engined low-wing plane, of metal construction and with very clean lines. It had a 1970-h.p. double-row radial engine and weighed only 3.5 tons unloaded, or just under 6 tons loaded and with fuel for 3000 miles. Its speed at 16,000 feet was not quite 400 m.p.h. As the Grumman Wildcat only did 320 m.p.h. and the Hellcat 380 m.p.h., there was no American carrier-borne plane capable of catching it. The Saiun—the word means 'many-coloured cloud'—was, in fact, a very successful plane.

The Shiden, or 'violet lightning', and better known by its code-name of 'George', came into service towards the end of 1944, like the Saiun. From then on it gradually began to replace the Zero as the standard front-line fighter.

Its production on a large scale was slowed down by the bombing of Kobe in January 1945, which destroyed the assembly plant. This was lucky for the Allies, as it was a tough customer. It had four cannon in the wings and two machine-guns firing through the propeller. Its rate of climb was 4250 feet a minute and its speed straight and level was 425 m.p.h. at 20,000 feet. It weighed 2.5 tons unloaded and could execute a 360-degree turn in ten seconds, just like the Zero. But unlike the Zero it had self-sealing tanks and a certain amount of armour-plating for the pilot.

It had a Homare 21 eighteen-cylinder double-row radial engine with two-stage supercharger and a four-bladed propeller. Its span was 39 feet 4 inches and its length 29 feet 3 inches, producing a very adequate wing area and a ridiculously low wing loading, a guarantee of excellent manoeuvrability.

Unlike the Zero, the George was a land-plane, not equipped for operating from aircraft-carriers. This detail shows how the situation for Japan had changed since 1942. Then the Japanese were very much on the offensive and had nothing but carrier-borne fighters. In 1944 the grip of the American task-forces had tightened and the bombing of the Japanese mainland was getting more severe. Japan could only be defended from bases on her own soil.

THE END

Milton Keynes UK
Ingram Content Group UK Ltd.
UKHW042145031224
452078UK00004B/458